CW00719833

COLLINS
GEM

MICRO FACTS
ZX
SPECTRUM

COLLINS
GEM

MICRO FACTS
ZX SPECTRUM

P.K. McBride
A.E. Weber

Collins
London and Glasgow

First published 1985
Reprint 10 9 8 7 6 5 4 3 2 1

© William Collins Sons & Co. Ltd. 1985

ISBN 0 00 458860-6

Phototypeset and illustrated by
Parkway Group, London and Abingdon

Printed in Great Britain by
Collins Clear-Type Press, Glasgow

Foreword

The ZX Spectrum has proved itself to be an ideal machine for beginners and advanced computer users alike. Sinclair BASIC is one of the most comprehensive and 'user-friendly' versions of the language around today. Its easy-to-use high-resolution graphics, colour and sound handling commands allow bright and colourful programs to be written by the relative novice, yet its text and number-processing capacities mean that it can be put to good use in serious commercial applications.

The Spectrum's microprocessor is a Z80A, an improved version of the widely-used Z80 chip, and it is controlled by industry-standard Z80 machine code instructions. This means that coding techniques learnt on the Spectrum can be applied to a great range of home and business computers.

This 'Micro Facts' is intended as a comprehensive reference guide for the Spectrum programmer. All BASIC instructions are included, usually with a short routine to demonstrate their use. The Z80 machine code instructions are also fully covered and a table of the mnemonics is given.

It also looks at the Spectrum hardware and operating system, and BASIC and machine code programming techniques.

As far as possible, jargon has been avoided, but where specialized terms are needed, they are used, and explained elsewhere under their own entries. Where a word is printed in bold in the text, it indicates that an entry can be found for it.

All entries are arranged in alphabetical order, so finding the reference for a BASIC or code instruction will present no problem. Tracking down references for programming techniques can take a little longer, as the words which people use to label techniques are not fully standardized. Cross-referencing (**bold print**) should help in this. Thus, if the reader wanted to look up methods for sorting data into order, he might start at 'alphabetical order'. Aspects of sorting are covered there, and, just as importantly, references are given to '**sort**' and '**bubble sort**' where actual routines are listed.

Machine code entries are centred on the

entry 'machine code'. References there will lead the reader to the next major entries, and from these further references will take him on to more detailed entries.

The basic rule for finding information in this book is to look under the most obvious word. If that fails – and it may only be 'obvious' to you – then try a related word.

The terms Sinclair, Spectrum, and ZX, and all combinations and derivatives of them, are Registered Trade Marks of Sinclair Research Limited.

abs

ABS A function (E Mode on ![G]). ABS returns the absolute value of a number, or of a numeric **argument**, by stripping off any negative sign.

    PRINT ABS −99

will give you '99'. This function finds the absolute difference between two numeric variables, when the larger is not known in advance.

    10 INPUT x
    20 INPUT y
    30 PRINT ABS (x−y)
    40 PRINT ABS (y−x)

This will print the same · positive number twice, no matter what values are entered.

absolute address The **address** that is given to a memory location by the Spectrum's hardware. The lowest address is ∅, at the start of **ROM** and the highest is 65535 in the 48K machine (32767 in the 16K version), at the top of **RAM**. The first address in RAM is 16384, the start of the **display file** which manages the screen.

See **address**.

accumulator The most important of all
the registers in the Z80 microprocessor, the
accumulator (the A register) is an 8-bit register. Almost all processing instructions (e.g.,
ADD, AND or CP) use the A register. Also,
much of the data that is passed to and from
different memory locations comes through it.
When the Z80 adds two single byte numbers,
the first is placed there, and the second added
in. The result is stored back in the accumulator. A **machine code** routine to add 2 and 2
could look like this:

```
LD   A,2   Put 2 in the accumulator
LD   B,2   Put 2 in the B register
ADD  B     Add the number in B to the
           number in the accumulator
LD   C,A   Put the result in the C register and
           . . .
LD   B,0   Clear B
RET        Return to BASIC
```

If this routine is called with 'PRINT USR. . .'
then the contents of the BC register pair (the
answer) will be displayed.

  See **machine code; registers**.

accuracy Translating between number systems (the Spectrum actually works in **binary**, although the results are displayed in decimal) inevitably means some loss of accuracy, but not usually enough to cause any problems. The first nine digits of any number and ten digit numbers up to 4 294 967 295 (2^{32} − 1) can be stored with complete accuracy. Above this, rounding can cause errors on the tenth digit with a loss of accuracy of up to .0000000002%. In accountancy terms, this is equivalent to 1p in £50 000 000·00. Problems can also creep in with smaller numbers where minute rounding errors can have a cumulative effect. e.g.:

```
10  LET x=0.01
20  LET y=0
30  LET y=y+x
40  PRINT y
50  IF y=4 THEN STOP
60  GOTO 30
```

When the program reaches 3.27, the next number it prints out is not 3.28 as expected, but 3.2799999. This error is then carried forward, so that the condition in line 50 is never met. Guard against bugs arising from this kind of situation by using the ABS function in condition testing:

   50 IF ABS (y−4)<.01 THEN STOP

See **INT** for another way of coping with rounding errors.

ACS A function (E Mode, SYMBOL SHIFT and ![W]). The ArcCoSine function is the reverse of the COSine, returning the angle (in **radians**) given by a cosine.

  See **trigonometry**.

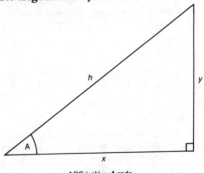

ACS (*x/h*) = A rads

ADC A Z80 instruction mnemonic, AdD with Carry. Acts on the accumulator or the HL register pair. ADC A,4 will add the status of the carry flag and 4 to the accumulator. If the carry flag is set to logic 1 and the accumulator held 5 then after the execution of the 'ADC A,4' instruction the accumulator will hold 1∅. If the carry flag was set to logic ∅ then the result would be 9.

See **condition testing**.

flag register

Mnemonic	Operand	Bytes	Clock cycle	S	Z		H		P/O	N	C
ADC	A, data	2	7	$	$		$		OV	0	$
ADC	A, register	1	4	$	$		$		OV	0	$
ADC	A, (HL)	1	7	$	$		$		OV	0	$
ADC	A, (index registers +displacement)	3	19	$	$		$		OV	0	$
ADC	HL, register pair	2	15	$	$		$		OV	0	$

ADD A Z80 instruction mnemonic. Like ADC, but the carry flag is not added to the accumulator, HL register pair or index registers.

See **condition testing**.

add

flag register

Mnem-onic	Operand	Bytes	Clock cycle	S	Z	H	P/O	N	C
ADD	A, data	2	7	$	$	$	OV	0	$
ADD	A, register	1	4	$	$	$	OV	0	$
ADD	A, (HL)	1	7	$	$	$	OV	0	$
ADD	A, (index registers + displacement)	3	19	$	$	$	OV	0	$
ADD	HL, register pair	1	11			$		0	$
ADD	index register, register pair	2	15			$		0	$

address The 48K Spectrum has a total of 64K of memory, 16K ROM + 48K RAM, giving 64 * 1024 locations in which data can be stored. Each location is identified by a number – its address – ranging from Ø to 65535. The 64K limit is not arbitrary. It arises from the fact that the largest number which can be held in two bytes is 65535 – in binary, 1111111111111111.

See **absolute address**.

address bus The Spectrum's central processing unit has a 16-wire (or bit) connection, each one of which can be set to logic Ø or logic 1. This enables the CPU to address any of 65536 (64K) memory locations individually.

addressing In Z80 machine code programming there are several addressing modes. These are **block transfer**, **extended addressing**, **immediate addressing**, **index addressing**, **register addressing**, **register indirect addressing**, **stack** and **zero page**.

algorithm A procedure which is followed to solve a particular type of problem. This can be written down as a series of steps, so that the algorithm for finding the biggest from a given set of numbers might look like this:

(1) set up a variable called 'biggest' and give it the value 'Ø'.

(2) take each number in turn and compare it with 'biggest'.

(3) if the number is larger, then give its value to 'biggest'.

(4) at the end of the set print out 'biggest'.

This translates into the following BASIC program, where the numbers are held in the array n(1Ø):

```
100   LET biggest=0
110   FOR i=1 to 10
120   IF n(i)>biggest THEN LET biggest=n(i)
```

```
130  NEXT i
140  PRINT biggest
```

alphabetical order This can be imposed on unorganized data by several methods. (*See* **bubble sort** and **sort**.) Whatever the method, the basis lies in the **ASCII** codes where 65 is the code for 'A', 66 for 'B' and so on. Strings can be compared using the arithmetical operators '>', '<', and '='. 'A' is less than 'B' because its code is lower. The length of the strings is irrelevant, so that 'Banking' comes before 'Bill', as the second letter of 'Banking' has a lower code than the equivalent letter in 'Bill'.

The case of the letters is relevant. Upper case letters (capitals) have ASCII codes between 65 and 90, while the lower case letters run from 97 to 122. If the entries in this dictionary had been arranged by the computer, then they would have begun 'ABS', 'ACS', 'ADC', 'ADD', 'AND', 'ASCII' etc. before coming to 'absolute address'.

AND A logical operator (SYMBOL SHIFT and **Y**). (1) In BASIC, the AND operator is used where it is necessary to test two or more conditions at the same time.

    ... IF first=9 AND second=9 AND third=9 THEN PRINT "Emergency"

The message will only appear if all three numbers are '9'.

In the priority of operations, AND comes before OR, and after NOT. AND can also be used in the sense of 'if the following condition is true'.

```
10  INPUT n$
20  PRINT ("Hi John" AND n$="John")
```

Here line 20 is the equivalent of '..IF n$= John" THEN PRINT "Hi John"..'. The real value of using AND in this way is that it allows you to embed conditions in lines, giving more compact programming.

```
PRINT TAB 10;(" " AND number<10);
number
```

This line will produce a neatly aligned tabular display of single and double-digit numbers:

    8
   12
    7
   23

(2) A Z80 instruction mnemonic: boolean instruction 'AND register'. Acts on the accumulator and logically ANDs the accumulator with data, e.g. 'AND A,30' will logically AND the contents of the accumulator with 30. AND can be used to test or alter the individual bits in a number. It compares each bit in a number with the equivalent bit in another number. If both are equal to one then is sets the bit in the answer to logic 1. Otherwise – if one or both bits equal logic 0 – it returns a value of logic 0. AND is often used in this way to **mask** one or more bits in a number. For example to find out what the bottom 4 bits in 213 are, AND it with 15. In binary 15 is 00001111. Thus the first 4 bits of 213 will be ignored since they are being compared with logic 0.

flag register

Mnemonic	Operand	Bytes	Clock cycle	S	Z		H		P/O	N	C
AND	data	2	7	$	$		1		P	0	0
AND	register	1	4	$	$		1		P	0	0
AND	(HL)	1	7	$	$		1		P	0	0
AND	(index registers + displacement)	3	19	$	$		1		P	0	0

See **truth tables**.

apostrophe A **PRINT** separator (SYM-BOL SHIFT and **7**). An apostrophe in a PRINT line will force a carriage return, pushing the PRINT position to the start of the next line.

    PRINT ' "Line 1" ' "Line 3". .

has the same effect as:

    PRINT : PRINT "Line 1": PRINT : PRINT "Line 3"

If several apostrophes are used together, then wider spacing will result.

argument The value, numeric or string, given to a function for processing. In 'CODE "a"' the argument is '"a"'. In 'ATTR (10,15)',10 and 15 are both arguments. An argument can be a **variable**, a number or a literal **string**.

arithmetic

SYMBOL SHIFT and	ADDITION	K	+
	SUBTRACTION	J	−
	MULTIPLICATION	B	*

SYMBOL SHIFT and	DIVISION	V	/
	BRACKETS	8	(
		9	)

In arithmetical operations on the Spectrum, normal rules of priority apply, so that $*$ and / have priority over $+$ and $-$. If brackets are used, then the operation inside them is carried out first. Brackets can be nested, with the innermost expressions being evaluated first, e.g.:

$$2 + 2 * 3 - 4 / 2 + 6 = 12$$
$$(2 + 2) * 3 - 4 / (2 + 6) = 11.5$$
$$(2 + 2) * ((3 - 4) / 2 + 6) = 22$$

arithmetic logic unit (ALU) The part of the central processing unit where addition, subtraction and logical operations are carried out.

array (or **arrayed variable**) Sometimes regarded as the most powerful tool at the programmer's disposal, the array allows masses of data to be handled in a simple fashion. While a normal variable (numeric or string) can store only one item of data at any given time, an array can hold as many items as the programmer requires. A simple number array might take the form n(10). This is equivalent to a single list with 10 elements, each having the same variable name – n –, but with a different subscript to identify the individual elements – n(1), n(2), n(3). . .

n(10)	
n(1)	
n(2)	
n(3)	
n(4)	
n(5)	
n(6)	
n(7)	
n(8)	
n(9)	
n(10)	

n$(10,6)					
n$(1)					
n$(2)					
n$(3)					
n$(4)					
n$(5)					
n$(6)					
n$(7)					
n$(8)					
n$(9)					
n$(10)					

Arrays do not exist until they are created by a **DIM statement**, which establishes the dimensions of the array. 'DIM n(20)' creates a number array of 20 elements, each having an initial value of zero. This might be used for storing the results of a survey, e.g.:

```
10   DIM n(20)
20   FOR i=1 TO 20
30   INPUT n(i)
40   NEXT i
50   FOR i=1 TO 20
60   PRINT n(i)
70   NEXT i
```

Any type of operation can be carried out on the array while it is running through the loop. By adding the following lines, the total and mean of this set of numbers could be calculated:

```
45   LET total=0
65   LET total=total+n(i)
80   LET mean=total/20
90   PRINT "Total ";total,"Mean ";mean
```

'DIM s$(32)' would create a **string** array of 32 elements, each of a single character, and initially holding a space. Single character arrays are useful as flags, but more often, you will want the arrays to be capable of storing strings consisting of words or phrases. In this case, an extra dimension – the length of the strings must be given. 'DIM n$(20,25)' would store

20 names (for example) of up to 25 characters each. If the names are shorter than that, then the remaining spaces in the strings are filled with blanks:

```
10  DIM n$(20,25)
20  FOR i=1 TO 20
30  INPUT n$(i)
40  NEXT i
50  FOR i=1 TO 20
60  PRINT PAPER 6;n$(i)
70  NEXT i
```

By PRINTing the names on a yellow background, the length of the strings can be seen quite clearly.

Arrays can have any number of dimensions, so long as there is memory space enough to cope with them. Thus, 't(20,20,5)' would set up a table of 20 rows 20 columns, with 5 elements in each box. Such an array could not be created on a 16K Spectrum as each element in a number array demands 5 bytes of memory, and here there would be a total of 20*20*5 elements. String arrays take a single byte for each element.

See **DIM; flag**.

ASCII (American Standard Code for Information Interchange) The Spectrum character set follows the ASCII code for all numbers, letters and virtually all punctuation and symbols; i.e. those characters between code 32 (space) and 125 (right brace). Outside of this range, the characters are unique to the Spectrum. Because almost all printable characters, apart from graphics, are in common with the ASCII set, it is possible to link up a Spectrum to other peripherals, such as printers, which conform to the same standard.

See **CODE; CHR$; character set**.

ASN A function (E Mode SYMBOL SHIFT and ▮Q▮). The ArcSiNe is the inverse of the SINe function, returning the angle, in radians, produced by a given sine value.

See **trigonometry**.

ASN (y/h) = A rads

assembler A program which converts **assembly language** instructions into **machine code**. With an assembler you can write machine code programs using mnemonics instead of numbers. Assemblers use labels to calculate the addresses of **CALL** and **JP** instructions and the **relative addresses** of **JR** instructions. This requires a two-pass assembler. On the first pass, the assembler makes a table of all the labels and their addresses. On the second pass it calculates the relative addresses and then inserts the addresses from the labels into the machine code.

assembly language A low-level language in which each **machine code** instruction is represented by a mnemonic. Assembly language programs consist of **operators** and **operands**. Before a program written in assembly language can be executed it needs to be converted into machine code by an **assembler**.

assign To give a value to a variable, e.g. 'LET number=99' assigns the value 99 to the variable 'number'. 'READ n$. . .DATA

"Fred'" assigns "Fred" to the variable 'n$'.

AT (SYMBOL SHIFT and 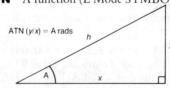). AT can be used in the PRINT lines to force the print position to a specific part of the screen. 'PRINT AT line, column; ". . .print items. . .". The line and column values must fall within the screen limits.

You can also print at a point in the bottom 2 lines of the screen by channelling data through **stream** 1:

PRINT #1; AT line, column;. . .

The line value here must be either Ø or 1. AT can also be used with INPUT to fix the position of the INPUT cursor. The choice of lines here is again to Ø or 1, as the INPUT must start in the lower part of the screen.

See opposite.

ATN A function (E Mode SYMBOL SHIFT

ATN (y/x) = A rads

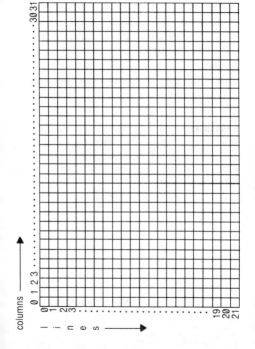

and ![E]). This is the ArcTaNgent – the reverse of the TANgent function, and it returns the angle, in radians, for a given tangent value.

See **trigonometry**.

ATTR A function (E Mode SYMBOL SHIFT and ![L]). This takes the form 'ATTR (line, column)' and returns the **attribute** code which is current at the given character space.

attribute The attributes of a character square govern the colour and brightness of any character printed at that point, or of any **high-resolution graphics** which pass through it. They cover not just PAPER and INK colours, but also BRIGHT and FLASH. The data is compressed into one byte per square using this formula:

Bit number	Decimal value	
7	128	FLASH – 128 if on
6	64	BRIGHT – 64 if on
5	32	
4	16	PAPER code ∗ 8
3	8	

Bit	Decimal
number	value
2	4
1	2 } INK code
0	1

Any square on the normal black on white screen would have the attribute code of 56 = $0+0+8*7+0$. A bright, flashing magenta character on a yellow background would have the code $220 = 128+64+8*3+4$. The attributes of the screen are held in a block of memory directly after the **display file**, and can be altered without affecting the graphics. The following routine would recolour the screen. Extra lines could be added so that FLASH and BRIGHT options became available to the user.

```
100   LET code=0
110   INPUT "Paper colour number? ";pcn
120   INPUT "Ink colour number? ";icn
130   LET code=code+8*pcn+icn
140   FOR a=22528 TO 23295
150   POKE a,code
160   NEXT a
```

Set the initial value of 'code' to '64' to turn 'BRIGHT' on, '128' for 'FLASH', and '192' for 'FLASH and BRIGHT'.

BASIC Beginner's All-purpose Symbolic Instruction Code was developed in America in the early 1960s as a simple introduction to programming. BASIC programs can be keyed in and tested one line at a time, as each instruction is interpreted (converted to code) and executed singly. This contrasts sharply with most other high-level languages, where the entire program is compiled into a block of code before execution. A number of dialects of BASIC have been developed, and of these, Sinclair BASIC is one of the 'friendliest' to use.

baud rate This refers to the speed at which data is transferred between the computer and peripheral devices, measured in bits per second. This can vary from 50 to 19 200 depending upon the device. Data is transferred to and from tape at 1500 baud, but with a microdrive, the rate can be up to 9600.

BCD (Binary Coded Decimal) Decimal numbers stored as binary digits. On the Z80, arithmetic operations are usually made in **hex-adecimal**. However, decimal calculations can be made using BCD numbers. Each decimal digit is represented in BCD form by 4 bits, e.g. 36 in BCD is 00110110:

```
0011  0110
3     6
```

By this method a byte can store a number from 0 to 99. When the Z80 microprocessor has been put in decimal mode by a **DAA** instruction, it adds and subtracts numbers in BCD form. In binary, 4 bits can store a number from 0 to 15. BCD is therefore less efficient in using memory space. For this reason it is rarely used except in certain business and scientific applications.

BEEP A statement (E Mode SYMBOL SHIFT and **Z**). 'BEEP time, pitch' sends a sound to the speaker for a time given in seconds, at a pitch measured in semitones from middle C. Thus:

```
BEEP 1,5
```

gives one second of the F above middle C.

As the sound is produced by a rather small

speaker, the quality of the notes is not very good, and it deteriorates the further you get from the middle ranges. The BEEPs are also output through the EAR and MIC sockets, and if an amplifier is connected to one of these, then reasonable quality notes can be obtained over a span of ten octaves – pitch values from -60 to $+60$.

The pitch values do not have to be whole numbers – indeed a little fine tuning is necessary if you have a sensitive musical ear.

    BEEP 1,2.04

will give a more accurate 'D' (in the key of C), than the simpler 'BEEP 1,2'

	Note	Pitch value
	G	7
	F	5
	E	4
	D	2
middle	C	0
	B	-1
	A	-3
	G	-5

Add 12 to raise a note by an octave, or subtract 12 for the octave below.

See **sounds**.

benchmarks Standard operations by which the speed of computers can be measured and compared. Typical benchmark tests are the empty loop, and the incrementing loop.

    FOR i=1 TO 1000: NEXT i
    FOR i=1 TO 1000: LET x=x+1: NEXT i

These take 4.16 and 7.38 seconds respectively.

BIN (E Mode **B**). This allows numbers to be given to the Spectrum in binary, rather than decimal, form. When **user defined graphics** are being created, BIN gives a simple method of transferring a design from squared paper to the computer.

    01111110
    10000001
    10100101
    10000001
    10100101
    10111101
    10000001
    01111110

This definition can now be given to one of the

user-defined characters, e.g. 'A', as follows:

```
10  POKE USR "A",   BIN 01111110
20  POKE USR "A"+1, BIN 10000001
30  POKE USR "A"+2, BIN 10100101
40  POKE USR "A"+3, BIN 10000001
```
. . . etc

binary coded decimal   *See* **BCD**.

binary numbers   Numbers written in base 2, rather than the base 10 of **decimal numbers**. To know 'how many' is meant by a number, you have to look not only at the digits, but also at their position in the number, e.g.:

In base 10 '234' means $200 = 2 * 10 * 10$
$$+ \quad 30 = 3 * 10$$
$$+ \quad 4 = 4 * 1$$

The same digit is worth different amounts in different columns. Starting with face value in the rightmost place, the value increases by a factor of 10 with each shift to the left. The same principle applies in base 2, except that the value increases by a factor of 2 with each left shift. That there are only two possible digits (0 and 1), and that only the first eight places are relevant, make life easier.

place value	128	64	32	16	8	4	2	1
powers of 2	2^7	2^6	2^5	2^4	2^3	2^2	2^1	2^0
binary 10110110	1	0	1	1	0	1	1	0
	128 +	0 +	32 +	16 +	0 +	4 +	2 +	0

$$= 182$$

Computers use binary numbers because 1 and 0 can be simply represented by the presence or absence of current. Think of a **bit** as a switch, and a set of 8 bits (a **byte**) as a bank of such switches, and you can see that any decimal number between 0 and 255 can be represented by setting those switches to on or off.

Binary addition follows the same rules as decimal addition:

```
   13     00001101 = 0+0+0+0+8+4+2+1
    9+    00001001 = 0+0+0+0+8+0+0+1
 = 22     00010110 = 0+0+0+16+0+4+2+0
            ↑  ↑
          carry 1
```

Subtraction is handled differently (*See* **two's complement**).

bit (BInary digiT)   The 8 bits of a **byte** are numbered 0 to 7 (from right to left). In some of the Spectrum's operations, individual bits are used to indicate the status of certain conditions. Thus, in a byte in attribute memory, bit 7 signals whether or not the related character square should 'FLASH' and bit 6 flags 'BRIGHT'.

BIT A Z80 instruction mnemonic. This tests whether a specified bit is set in one of the A,B,C,D,E,H or L registers. The format of the instruction is 'BIT n, register' where n is the bit number Ø–7. 'BIT 4,C' will test bit 4 of the C register. If this bit is set to logic 1 then the zero flag will be set to logic 1 – otherwise it will be set to logic Ø. Register indirect 'BIT n, (HL)' and index addressing modes 'BIT n, (IX+displacement)' are available with this instruction.

flag register

Mnem-onic	Operand	Bytes	Clock cycle	S	Z		H		P/O	N	C
BIT	bit, register	2	8	?	$		1		?	0	
BIT	bit, (HL)	2	12	?	$		1		?	0	
BIT	bit, (index registers +displacement)	4	20	?	$		1		?	0	

block transfer An addressing mode in which data is transferred from one memory location to another or it is searched for.

See **CPD**; **CPDR**; **CPI**; **CPIR**; **IND**; **INDR**; **INI**; **INIR**; **LDD**; **LDDR**; **LDI**; **LDIR**; **OTDR**; **OTIR**; **OUTD**; **OUTI**.

boolean instruction (from boolean algebra) An operation involving **AND**, **OR** or **XOR** instructions, the results of which can be shown in a **truth table**.

BORDCR A system variable, address 23624. BORDCR holds the **attributes** for the border area, including the bottom two lines of the main screen, but changing this before an INPUT will at first only affect the lower screen. Use it to create a 'window' in the INPUT area.

When POKEing this variable, multiply the code for the border colour by 8, and add in the INK code, e.g.:

POKE 23624,39: INPUT "Answer";a$

This will produce green PAPER and white INK in the INPUT area.

Adding in the normal attribute codes will make the lower screen BRIGHT or FLASHing, though only the PAPER colour of the border can be changed.

BORDER A statement (keyword on **B**). BORDER followed by a numerical argument in the range Ø to 7 sets the colour of the border of the screen, and the bottom 2 lines of the main screen. The numerical argument can be a number, a number variable, or an expression:

```
LET b=2: BORDER 2 : BORDER b :
BORDER (b+2)/2
```

In every case the border colour will be set to red.

bracket Characters which come in three varieties: square brackets and curly brackets (also known as braces) are simply printable characters; only the round brackets have any place in program statements.

Square	E Mode	SYMBOL SHIFT	Y	[
	"	"	U	]
Curly (Braces)	"	"	F	{
	"	"	G	}
Round		"	8	(
		"	9	)

When evaluating an arithmetical or logical expression, the Spectrum will tackle bracketted sections first. Brackets can be nested as deeply need be.

branch   This is a point in a program where the flow is, or can be, redirected. The branch is usually conditional, with two or more alternative routes possible.

See **IF**.

BREAK   Pressing CAPS SHIFT and BREAK/SPACE will halt the execution of any BASIC program or command and display one of two error reports. 'D BREAK – CONT repeats' will be shown if the Spectrum was transferring data to or from cassette or a printer at the time. The report also occurs if 'N', 'SPACE' or 'STOP' are pressed when a 'scroll?' message appears during listing or other printing on the screen. CONT does not in fact repeat if a simple LIST command has been broken into.

'L BREAK into program' is displayed if a BREAK is forced during program execution. In this situation, **CONT** will restart the program at the next statement.

BREAK can be disabled in several ways – *see* **DF SZ**; **ERR SP**.

BRIGHT A statement (E Mode, SYMBOL SHIFT and **B**). Spectrum can print at two levels of brightness, normal (BRIGHT 0) and extra bright (BRIGHT 1). The border area is not affected by the BRIGHT statement.

This program shows the difference between normal and extra-bright colours:

```
10  BRIGHT 1
20  FOR i=0 TO 7
30  PAPER i: CLS
40  PAUSE 0
50  NEXT i
```

If BRIGHT is used within a PRINT line, it only affects the subsequent items in that line:

```
PRINT "dull";BRIGHT 1; "bright "
PRINT "what now?"
```

Where a combination of BRIGHT 0 and BRIGHT 1 printing has been used on a screen, then the statement 'BRIGHT 8' will cause all later items to take their level of brightness from the squares in which they are printed, in the same way that PAPER 8, or INK 8 allows 'transparent' printing.

bubble sort A method of sorting sets of numbers or strings into numerical or arithmetical order. The routine works by running repeatedly through the set, switching the values in any pair which are in the wrong order. In the worst possible case, the number of passes that must be made is equal to one less than the number of items in the set.

```
 10  DIM n(10)    Create an array to hold the
                                       numbers
 20  FOR i=1 TO 10
 30  INPUT n(i)   Collect ten numbers (any
                                       values)
 40  NEXT i
 50  LET flag=0   'Switch flag' used below
 60  FOR i=1 TO 9
 70  IF n(i)<=n(i+1) THEN GOTO 120
                    Right way round – skip
 80  LET x=n(i)    Transfer value to spare
 90  LET n(i)=n(i+1)         Begin switch
100  LET n(i+1)=x         Complete switch
110  LET flag=1   Show switch has occurred
```

```
120  NEXT i
130  FOR i=1 TO 10
140  PRINT n(i);" ";              Display routine
150  NEXT i
160  PRINT
170  IF flag=1 THEN GOTO 50
```

The display routine is purely for interest and would not normally be included. Alphabetical sorts follow exactly the same pattern, the sole difference being that a string array is used, and 'x$' replaces 'x' as the spare store.

See **sort**.

buffer   (1) Software buffer: an area of memory set aside for the temporary storage of data in the process of being transferred from one device or piece of software to another. Buffers are useful when slow peripheral devices are connected to the computer, because then the central processing unit is not kept waiting. The printer buffer on the Spectrum is a page set just above the attribute memory. Data is sent to the printer only when the buffer is full or when the very last bytes of data are to be printed. This leaves the computer free for other tasks until a next full page of data has to be sent again.

(2) Hardware buffer: a device put into a signal wire (e.g. **address bus**) to boost the signal.

bug A fault in a program or in the operating system. There are no significant bugs in the Spectrum's hardware, though they frequently occur in programs. *See* **debugging** for advice on how to deal with them.

bus *See* **address bus; data bus**.

byte The basic unit in computing. The Spectrum is an 8-bit computer, so a byte consists of 8 bits and can store integers between 0 and 255. Each of the Spectrum's 65536 memory locations can hold one byte of data.

calculated GO SUBs, GO TOs. Some dialects of BASIC have an 'ON variable GO TO. . .' statement which allows for easy re-direction of program flow. In them a line like this might be used in a menu selection routine:

```
ON choice GO SUB 1000,2000,3000,4000
```

It directs the program to the subroutine at 1000 for option 1, 2000 for option 2, etc.

There is no such statement in Sinclair BASIC, but the same effect can be achieved by the use of calculated GO SUBs or GO TOs:

```
GO SUB choice*1000
GO TO 1000 + choice * 100
```

The calculation can be as complex as need be, so long as it results in a number. If the Spectrum is sent to a line number that does not exist, it will carry on down to the next line.

CALL A Z80 instruction mnemonic. This instruction takes the form 'CALL address' and will jump to a subroutine at a specified 16-bit address. When this instruction is executed the address of the next instruction after the CALL is PUSHed onto the central processing unit stack and the CALLed address is put into the **program counter**. At the end of the CALLed subroutine a RET instruction will POP the stack into the program counter. The next instruction after the CALL instruction will then be executed. A CALL to a subroutine can also be made with certain conditions to be satisfied – 'CALL C,address', 'CALL NC,address', 'CALL M,address', 'CALL P,address',

'CALL Z,address' 'CALL NZ,address',
'CALL PE,address', 'CALL PO,address'
CALL does not affect the flag register.

See **condition testing**.

flag register

Mnem-onic	Operand	Bytes	Clock cycle	S	Z		H		P/O	N	C
CALL	address	3	17								
CALL	condition, address	3	10/17*								

* First clock cycle for 'condition not met', the second for 'condition met'.

CAPS LOCK (CAPS SHIFT and **2**). The switch between C mode (capitals) and L mode (lower case).

carry flag *See* **flag register**.

cassette use The cassette recorder can be used to SAVE and LOAD programs, blocks of code, data files and screens, and provides a safe and convenient storage medium. Most types of cassette recorder are suitable, and any reasonable quality audio tape will work as well as the special computer tapes. The strong signal generated by the Spectrum helps to ensure good recordings. Short tapes (10 or 12 min.) are most convenient to handle, and if possible they should only have one program per side. If several programs are stored on the same tape then the tape counter numbers should be noted carefully.

When SAVEing programs or data, only the MIC lead should be connected, as feedback through the EAR lead can corrupt the recording.

See **SAVE**; **LOAD**; **VERIFY**; **MERGE**.

CAT can only be used with the **microdrive**. It gives a CATalogue (list) of the files on the cartridge in a given drive. 'CAT 1' would refer to drive 1, and the list would be displayed on the television screen.

CCF A Z80 instruction mnemonic: Complement Carry Flag. To complement a flag is to change its status. If the carry flag status was logic 1 then CCF will change it to logic $\emptyset$ and *vice versa*.

flag register

Mnemonic	Operand	Bytes	Clock cycle	S	Z		H		P/O	N	C
CCF		1	4				?			$\emptyset$	$

central processing unit (CPU) The Spectrum uses a Z80A **microprocessor** and it is the most important part of the computer. The CPU is made up of a control unit, instruction register, program counter, arithmetic logic unit and 21 user registers.

channel The Spectrum can send DATA to devices specified by the channel number. The RS232 interface, the network and keyboard are channels that data can come from. The printer, television screen and microdrive are channels that data can be sent to.

See **OPEN#; MOVE; CLOSE#**.

character A letter, digit, symbol or other graphic which will occupy one character space when printed on screen, and which can be held in a single byte in memory.

character set The codes 0 to 31 produce either non-printable characters, or are not used. Codes 165 to 255 are 'tokens'. Only 32 to 164 produce single printing symbols.

See overleaf

Code	Character	Code	Character	Code	Character
32	space	58	:	84	T
33	!	59	;	85	U
34	"	60	<	86	V
35	#	61	=	87	W
36	$	62	>	88	X
37	%	63	?	89	Y
38	&	64	@	90	Z
39	'	65	A	91	[
40	(	66	B	92	\
41	)	67	C	93	]
42	*	68	D	94	↑
43	+	69	E	95	—
44	,	70	F	96	£
45	–	71	G	97	a
46	.	72	H	98	b
47	/	73	I	99	c
48	0	74	J	100	d
49	1	75	K	101	e
50	2	76	L	102	f
51	3	77	M	103	g
52	4	78	N	104	h
53	5	79	O	105	i
54	6	80	P	106	j
55	7	81	Q	107	k
56	8	82	R	108	l
57	9	83	S	109	m

Code	Character	Code	Character	Code	Character
110	n	129	◨	148	E ⎤
111	o	130	◪	149	F
112	p	131	▬	150	G
113	q	132	◰	151	H
114	r	133	◫	152	I
115	s	134	◩	153	J
116	t	135	◧	154	K
117	u	136	◨	155	L
118	v	137	◪	156	M
119	w	138	◧	157	N
120	x	139	◪	158	O
121	y	140	▬	159	P
122	z	141	◧	160	Q
123	{	142	◪	161	R
124	|	143	■	162	S
125	}	144	A ⎤	163	T
126	~	145	B	164	U ⎦
127	©	146	C		
128	□	147	D ⎦		

user definable graphics

CHARS A system variable: address 23606-7. It normally points to 15360 which is 256 bytes less than the address of the character set. The pattern of any character, except block and user defined graphics, can be seen by using this

routine:
```
10  INPUT "Character ?";c$
20  LET address = 15360+8 * CODE c$
30  FOR i=0 TO 7
40  PRINT PEEK (address+i)
50  NEXT i
```
The Spectrum uses a similar routine to obtain its character data, and as the first printable character is 'space' (CODE 32), then its data will be found at 15360+256 (32*8).

This character data is in ROM and cannot therefore be changed, but CHARS can be made to point at an address in RAM where an alternative character set could be defined.

CHR\$ A function (E Mode **U**). It converts an **ASCII** code to a character, and can be used to gain access to the **non-printable characters**.
```
IF INKEY$ = CHR$ 13 THEN PRINT
"You pressed ENTER"
IF INKEY$ = CHR$ 12 THEN PRINT
"That's DELETE"
```
CHR$ might be used in a routine to impose a standard format on an INPUT. This puts

names into lower case, with capital first letters:
'PETER' and 'peter' would both be converted
to 'Peter'.

```
100  INPUT n$
110  IF n$(1)>"Z" THEN LET n$(1)=CHR$
     (CODE n$(1)-32)
120  FOR i=2 TO LEN n$
130  IF n$(i)<"a" THEN LET n$(i)=CHR$
     (CODE n$(i)+32)
140  NEXT i
150  PRINT "Hello ";n$
```

CIRCLE   A statement (E Mode, SYMBOL
SHIFT and **H**). 'CIRCLE' must be followed
by the x,y co-ordinates of the centre, and the
radius. 'CIRCLE 128,88,50' will draw a circle,
radius 50 pixels, at the centre of the screen.

A solid circle can be produced by running
the radius value through a loop.

```
10  FOR r=1 TO 50
20  CIRCLE 128,88,r
30  NEXT r
```

If the CIRCLE runs off-screen, a crash will
occur. However, crash-proof circles can be
drawn using the trigonometrical functions.

```
10   INPUT "x value? ";x
20   INPUT "y value? ";y
30   INPUT "radius? ";r
40   FOR a=0 TO 2*PI STEP 1/r
50   LET x1=SIN a*r+x: LET y1=COS
     a*r+y
60   IF x1>=0 AND x1<=255 AND y1>=0
     AND y1<=175 THEN PLOT x1,y1
70   NEXT a
```

Obviously, this is slower than the CIRCLE statement.

CLEAR A statement (keyword on **X**). (1) Used by itself, this statement erases all variables, including arrays, clears the GO SUB stack and performs **RESTORE** and **CLS**. In the process it frees the memory space that the variables had occupied, and this is sometimes useful. When developing a very long program it is sometimes impossible to EDIT long lines, or even to replace them. CLEAR performed before editing should create some free space in which to work. (2) 'CLEAR' followed by a number resets **RAMTOP** to the number given (as long as it is within the available RAM area). The memory above RAMTOP can then be used for machine code routines, or for storing the data for an alternative character set.

clock (or clock-pulse generator) The circuit which controls the speed at which the Z80A central processing unit chip operates (3.5 million pulses per second, or 3.5 Mega-Hertz). As many of the CPU's actions involve several operations, the Spectrum normally carries out about half a million machine code instructions per second. While the 'clock' is not accessible, another timer – the **FRAMES** system variable – can be used to set up timing routines.

CLOSE# A statement (E Mode, SYMBOL SHIFT and **5**). The command takes the format 'CLOSE# stream', and unlinks any channel from the named **stream**. It is important to CLOSE# an OPENed microdrive or network file after use. This is because data is only saved when the device **buffer** is full. Closing a file ensures that a partly filled buffer is saved.

CLS A statement (keyword on **V**). It CLears the Screen, wiping the display file, and resetting the whole of **attribute** memory to whatever value is then current. The PRINT position is restored to the top left, and the PLOT position to the bottom left.

```
10  PAPER 7: CLS
20  PAPER 5: PRINT "testing"
30  PAUSE 0: CLS
```

When developing a program in which a range of PAPER and INK colours are used, it is useful to add a line at the end:

```
9999 PAPER 7: INK 0: FLASH 0: CLS :
LIST
```

'GO TO 9999' will produce a readable listing no matter what colours had been in use.

C mode (capitals)   Indicated by C cursor. Pressing the letter keys gives upper case (capital) letters. To switch from C to L mode, press CAPS LOCK (CAPS SHIFT and **2**).

CODE   A function (E Mode **I**). (1) CODE returns the **ASCII** code of a given character, or of the first character in a longer string.

```
LET c$ = "F" : PRINT CODE "F", CODE
"Fred", CODE c$
```

will all return '70'.

In some situations, e.g. when using calculated GO SUBs, it may be useful to collect the character code from the keyboard, rather than the character.

```
LET z= CODE INKEY$: IF z=0 THEN
. . (wait)
GOSUB (z−48)∗1000. . .
```

(2) Used in SAVEing LOADing and VERIFYing **machine code** programs. CODE takes the form 'SAVE "filename" CODE address, length'. 'Address' is the start address of the program and 'length' is the number of bytes to be saved.

colon   Punctuation (SYMBOL SHIFT and **Z**). The colon is used to separate statements in a multi-statement line, either in a program or in direct mode.

```
FOR i=1 TO 20 : PRINT n(i): NEXT i
```

Used as a direct command this would print out the array 'n()' for checking.

The use of multi-statement lines does save some memory space – 4 bytes per line – but tends to reduce readability and ease of editing.

colour   The Spectrum has 8 colours, but

these can easily be doubled by the careful use of BRIGHT. There is a distinct difference between BRIGHT and normal colours, especially with the paler ones. Additional colours can be obtained through User Defined Graphics. Here a striped UDG is defined; this could be used for shading background areas:

```
10  FOR r=0 TO 7:
20  POKE USR "A"+r,85
30  NEXT r
40  INPUT "Paper? ";p
50  INPUT "Ink? ";i
60  PAPER p: INK i
70  FOR j=1 TO 10: PRINT "A";:NEXT j
80  GO TO 40
```

Some of the colours produced by speckled and striped UDG's are not very good as they tend to flicker.

Colours can be changed by the PAPER and INK commands, and by the use of the colour control characters.

See **INV VIDEO**.

colour control characters These are accessible from the keyboard. Where coloured printing is wanted, using colour control characters rather than **PAPER** and **INK** commands has the great advantage of making the lines stand out, and saves 7 bytes each time. To change the paper colour, press the SHIFT keys to go into **E Mode**, then press a number key (∅ to 7). To change the ink colour, go into E Mode, then hold down CAPS SHIFT while pressing a number key. **8** and **9** have slightly different properties. E Mode and **9** gives extra BRIGHT colours, while E Mode, CAPS SHIFT and **9** turns FLASH on. Use **8** instead of **9** to turn BRIGHT and FLASH off.

Program lines can be made invisible by using the same colour for ink and paper, but, as the controls can be deleted easily, this is next to useless as a form of program protection. It has more value in concealing individual lines, or parts of lines – perhaps those that contain the answers to quizzes. These colour controls take no apparent space in the program lines, though in fact each consists of two characters. This becomes clear when you try to delete them, or to move the cursor through them.

comma Punctuation (SYMBOL SHIFT and **N**). The comma is a separator. Used in program lines, it will separate the parameters of a function – ' PLOT x,y', or items of data – 'DATA "Fred",35,"male"'.

Used in PRINT lines, the comma pushes the print position to the start of the next print zone, which on a Spectrum is half a screen wide.

    PRINT 1,2,3,4,5,. . .

command A command is given directly to the machine without a line number, while an instruction is part of a program, and therefore has a number. Most **statements** can be used as commands.

comparisons These are made using the symbols '<', '>' and '=', either individually, or in the compound forms '<=', '>=', '<>'. The expression on either side of the symbol can be as complex as need be, so long as both sides are of the same type – numeric or string.

    IF VAL a$ ✳ VAL b$ = ans. . .
    IF n$(1)= CHR$(x(i,2)). . .

When strings are compared, they are equal if

they are of the same length and contain the same characters. This can create problems when comparing simple variables with the arrays. In this example, the array is a\$(1∅,1∅), and the comparison gives a negative result:

```
LET a$(1)="TEST":LET b$="TEST"
IF b$=a$(1) THEN. . .
```

If this problem is likely to occur, then write in lines to make the simple variable the same length as the arrayed string:

```
IF LEN b$>10 THEN LET b$=b$( TO 10)
IF LEN b$<10 THEN b$=b$+" ": GO TO
. .(start of line to repeat)
```

See **logical operators; procrustean assignment**.

compiler A program which converts a program written in a high-level language, such as PASCAL, into a block of machine code for execution. BASIC compilers can be obtained, though as BASIC was not intended to be a compiled language, there are usually limits on the types of programs that can be handled. BASIC compilers are normally unable to cope with string variables or arrays, and may have other limitations as well.

Compiled programs run at machine code speed, which is why they are favoured in commercial and scientific applications.

See **interpreter**.

complement *See* **two's complement**.

composite video A type of video signal which allows a **monitor** to be used instead of a television. Normally the video output is fed through a modulator which raises the frequency of the signal so that it is equivalent to a UHF TV signal. Because composite video signals are not modulated but sent directly to the monitor they give a higher quality picture.

See **monitor**.

condition testing In Z80 machine code programming, the flags in the **flag register** are set after an **arithmetic**, **boolean** or **shift** operation. The flags can be then individually tested and acted on.

Jumps can be made (**JP**, **JR**) and subroutines CALLed and ended (**RET**) if you know how the flags are affected when an instruction is executed.

The conditions which can be tested are the following: parity even (PE); parity odd (PO); result zero (Z); result not zero (NZ); carry set (C); carry not set (NC); result positive (P); result negative (N).

CONT(INUE) A statement (keyword on **C**). This will restart a program after a BREAK (from the keyboard) or a STOP. Execution normally continues from the line after the STOP, or the statement after the one that was broken into.

Where the error report was 'H STOP in INPUT', then CONTINUE will repeat the INPUT statement. Execution of the interrupted statement will usually continue where the report was 'D BREAK - CONT repeats'
See **BREAK**.

control character In some BASIC dialects it is possible to move the cursor by using control characters. In Sinclair BASIC only CHR$ 8 (cursor left) has any effect. 'PRINT "ab";CHR$ 8;"c". . .' produces 'ac'
See **non-printable characters**.

control unit A unit that co-ordinates the timing of events for the **central processing unit**. It handles the CPU input, processing and output.

co-ordinates The Spectrum has co-ordinate sets for **high-resolution graphics**, and for character printing. The print co-ordinates are normally referred to by 'line' and 'column', with 22 lines numbered 0 to 21 downscreen, and 32 columns numbered 0 to 31 left to right. In high-resolution work, the horizontal and vertical co-ordinates are generally called 'x' and 'y'. The x co-ordinates are numbered 0 to 255, left to right, and the y co-ordinates 0 to 175, upscreen.

To convert x,y co-ordinates to line and column use these formulae:

line = 21 − INT (y/8)
column = INT (x/8)

The following formulae convert print co-ordinates to high resolution form, with x,y being at the centre of the character square.

x = column ∗ 8 + 4
y = (21-line) ∗ 8 + 4

See **high resolution graphics; AT**.

COPY A statement (keyword on **Z**). This produces a printer copy of the main screen, reproducing printed characters and high-resolution graphics. Blocks of coloured PAPER, that might form an important part of the screen display, will be left blank by the printer.

COS A function (E Mode, **W**). This returns the cosine of an angle given in radians.
See **trigonometry**.

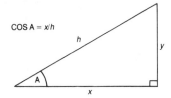

$$\text{COS A} = x/h$$

CP A Z80 mnemonic instruction. It compares the accumulator with registers B,C,D,E,H or L, data 'CP 30' or memory 'CP (HL), CP (IX+displacement)'. If the number in the accumulator is the same as the one with which it is compared, then the zero flag is set to logic 1. If it is smaller than the compared number, then the carry flag is set to logic 1. Otherwise it is set to logic Ø.

See **SUB; condition testing**.

				flag register					
Mnem-onic	Operand	Bytes	Clock cycle	S	Z	H	P/O	N	C
CP	data	2	7	$	$	$	OV	1	$
CP	register	1	4	$	$	$	OV	1	$
CP	(HL)	1	7	$	$	$	OV	1	$
CP	(index registers +displacement)	3	19	$	$	$	OV	1	$

CPD A Z80 instruction mnemonic: Compare the accumulator with memory and then Decrement HL and BC register pairs. The HL register pair holds the address of memory and the register pair is used as a counter. If the contents of the accumulator are equal to the memory location then the zero flag is set to logic 1. This instruction is useful for a byte search in memory. The BC register pair holds the range in which the search is to be carried out. The search can then be terminated by testing the zero flag or checking that the BC register pair reaches zero.

flag register

Mnem-onic	Operand	Bytes	Clock cycle	S	Z		H		P/O	N	C
CPD		2	16	$	$		$		$	1	

CPDR A Z80 instruction mnemonic: Com-Pare the accumulator with memory and De-crement HL and BC register pairs. The HL register pair holds the address of memory and the BC register pair is used as a counter. This instruction is like **CPD** except that it is Re-peated until the counter reaches zero or a match has been found.

flag register

Mnem-onic	Operand	Bytes	Clock cycle	S	Z		H		P/O	N	C
CPDR		2	20/16*	$	$		$		$	1	

* First clock cycle for 'condition not met', the second for 'condition met'.

CPI A Z80 instruction mnemonic: ComPare the accumulator with memory and Increment HL register pair and decrement BC register pair. The HL register pair holds the address of memory and the BC register pair is used as a counter.
See **CPD**.

flag register

Mnem-onic	Operand	Bytes	Clock cycle	S	Z		H		P/O	N	C
CPI		2	16	$	$		$		$		1

CPIR A Z80 instruction mnemonic: Compare the accumulator with memory, decrement BC register pair and Increment HL register pair. The HL register pair holds the address of memory and the BC register pair is used as a counter. This instruction is like **CPI** except that it is Repeated until the counter reaches zero or a match has been found.

See **CPDR**.

flag register

Mnem-onic	Operand	Bytes	Clock cycle	S	Z		H		P/O	N	C
CPIR		2	20/16	$	$		$		$		1

* First clock cycle for 'condition not met', the second for 'condition met'.

CPL A Z80 instruction mnemonic: Complement the accumulator. Each bit in the accumulator is complemented. If the bits in the accumulator are 10101010, then after this instruction they will be 01010101.

flag register

Mnem-onic	Operand	Bytes	Clock cycle	S	Z		H		P/O	N	C
CPL		1	4				1				1

CPU *See* **central processing unit**.

crash-proof Routines are crash-proof when nothing that a user can do will cause an error report to be generated. Making INPUT routines secure, and checking that variables remain within acceptable limits, should be the first stages in crash-proofing a program.

current line The line which was last entered, or which was specified in a LIST command. The current line can be identified by the program cursor ▷ between the line number and the first statement. If CAPS SHIFT and **1** (EDIT) are pressed, this is the line which will be copied into the workspace at the bottom of the screen. The current line can be changed by reLISTing, or by moving the cursor with CAPS SHIFT and **7** (for up) or **6** (for down).

cursors The Spectrum has two cursors.

The program cursor indicates the current line, and is always **>**. The second cursor will take different forms, depending upon the **mode** in force at the time:

K – keyword mode.

L – letter mode.

C – capitals mode.

G – graphics mode.

E – extended mode.

DAA A Z80 instruction mnemonic: Decimal Adjust Accumulator. The contents of the accumulator are converted to binary-coded decimal form. This instruction should only be used after additions and subtractions.

See **BCD**.

flag register

Mnem-onic	Operand	Bytes	Clock cycle	S	Z		H		P/O	N	C
DAA		1	4	$	$		$		P		$

data A general term to cover any form of information given to the computer either through **INPUT**, **LET** statements or **DATA** lines.

DATA   A statement (E Mode **D**). DATA in
a program identifies a line containing data to
be **READ** by the program. The items in the
DATA list must be separated by commas, and
any strings must be enclosed in quotation
marks. Where a mixture of numeric and string
data is needed, care must be taken to ensure
that the data will be READ into the right type
of variable.

Data lines can be included anywhere in a
program, and readability may be improved by
putting the data close to the routine to which it
relates. However, putting all data at the end of
the program will improve running times, as
the BASIC interpreter has to scan the program
from the first line every time the flow is
redirected by a GO TO or GO SUB. The
fewer lines which have to be scanned, the
faster the program can run. The system variable DATADD points to the last item of data
that was READ.

   See **RESTORE**.

database   A collection of **data** stored in a
computer or peripheral device which can be

interrogated, sorted or updated. In a standard commercial system, the database might hold data about stocks, salaries, sales, bills, production, etc. This data would normally be arranged so that it could be used by a variety of related programs which prepare invoices, handle stock control and keep the sales ledger.

data bus The Spectrum's central processing unit has a set of 8 wires over which all data transactions between it and other devices take place. The **address bus** holds the memory location into which the data bus can read or write byte information.

data processing The term tends to be reserved for business programs, but in fact everything the computer does is a form of data processing – storing, sifting, manipulating, transferring and displaying.

debugging The longer the program, the more options you write into it, the more routes you create through it, the more flexibility you give to the user – and the longer debugging will take. The easiest bugs to cure

are the ones that never reach the machine, so
prepare thoroughly before keying in. Plan out
the program in **flowchart** form, and draw up
separate flowcharts for any sections that are
not straightforward. Write down the variables
you will use, their purpose, and the limits, if
any, that they must observe. Sketch out the
screens on squared paper and check that the
information to be displayed will fit in the space
available. Plan how to arrange any DATA that
the program needs, and what RESTOREs will
be needed to get the right data READ into the
right variables. The ideal program requires no
debugging, because it has been planned to the
last detail. Unfortunately, very few people
write ideal programs.

When debugging, use the error reports to
the full. They will pinpoint the statement in
which the crash occurs, so check that statement carefully. The error may be very obvious
– a misspelt variable, or a wrong line number
for a GO TO or GO SUB. Print out the values
of the variables in the statement and compare
them with what you would expect to find
there. If the problem arises from a variable,

then trace its route back through the program, or write in a series of lines to print out its changing values. Returning from **sub-routines** is another frequent cause of error. Every GO SUB must be matched by a RE-TURN. Where subroutines are deeply nested, a misplaced GO TO can take a while to track down.

If possible, get a print-out of the program. It is much easier to trace faults if you can see the whole of the listing.

DEC A Z80 instruction mnemonic. DEC subtracts 1 from the contents of a specified register. If the register then contains Ø, the zero flag will be set to logic 1. Otherwise it will be

flag register

Mnem-onic	Operand	Bytes	Clock cycle	S	Z	H	P/O	N	C
DEC	register	1	4	$	$	$	OV	1	
DEC	register pair	1	6						
DEC	index registers	2	10						
DEC	(HL)	1	11	$	$	$	OV	1	
DEC	(index registers +displacement)	3	23	$	$	$	OV	1	

reset to logic ∅. DEC 'register pair' will not affect any of the flags.

See **condition testing**.

decimals   *See* **floating point binary**.

DEF FN   A statement (E Mode, SYMBOL SHIFT and **■1**). It allows you to DEFine FuNctions (numeric or string) to suit the needs of a program. The statement takes the form:

DEF FN name (argument)= equation

One or more variables may be included in the argument and the equation. Thus a function to find the character column in which a high-resolution point has been plotted will look like this:

DEF FN c(x) = INT (x/8)

The new function needs only to be called by name: 'PRINT TAB FN c( );. . .' is sufficient. It is not necessary to include the 'x' (assuming a variable called 'x' exists). A different variable, or a number could be given as the argument, and the function would still work:

. . .LET x1=200: PRINT FN c(x1): PRINT FN c(200)

Both would print '25'. The main use of DEF

FN is creating functions to cope with complex calculations which have to be performed frequently in the program. The following might be needed in a physics program concerned with the Gas Laws. It calculates a change in gas pressure.

    DEF FN n()=(p * v * h)/(t * q)

p, v and t are the original values for pressure, volume and temperature: h and q are the later temperature and volume figures.

    PRINT FN n( ). . .

displays the new pressure.

The DEF FN lines can be included anywhere in the program, but are best sited at the beginning. When the program meets FN, it searches the program for the definition before it executes the function. As the search starts at line 1, putting the definitions at the beginning improves running times.

degrees The Spectrum gives angles in **radians** not degrees. As 2 * PI (π) radians equals 360 degrees, the conversion formulae are:

    degrees = radians * 180/π
    radians = degrees * π/180

DELETE (CAPS SHIFT and ▣). 'DE-
LETE' erases that character or keyword to the
left of the cursor – normally the last one that
was typed. A line can be deleted by typing its
line number and pressing ENTER. The Spectrum removes the old line of that number to
make way for the new, realizes that the re-
placement line is empty and closes up the gap
instead. There is no way of reclaiming a line
deleted by mistake. It must be retyped.

DF SZ A system variable, address 23659.
This DeFines SiZe of the working space at the
bottom of the main screen. By poking '∅' into
this address you can disable the lower screen,
and thereby protect your programs from unau-
thorized entry. Any attempt to BREAK into
the program, so that it can be listed, will cause
a total crash, as the Spectrum is unable to print
its BREAK report. Unfortunately, the same
will happen with any attempt to use the lower
part of the screen, e.g. for INPUTs or for
editing. If you do intend to use this singularly
unfriendly method of program protection,
then do not add it until the end, and make sure

that you leave yourself an escape route – a password protected routine that will reset DF SZ to its proper value of 2.

DI A Z80 instruction mnemonic. It disables all maskable **interrupts**. The keyboard is scanned by the Spectrum every 1/50th second by a maskable interrupt routine. All maskable interrupts are turned off during a SAVE or when a BEEP is made. This has the effect of disabling the keyboard. These interrupts are enabled again with the instruction 'EI'.

flag register

Mnem-onic	Operand	Bytes	Clock cycle	S	Z		H •		P/O	N	C
DI		1	4								

DIM A statement (keyword on **D**). It is used to set up an **array**. The statement takes the form:

DIM name(dimensions)

The 'name' must be a single letter, or a single letter followed by '$' for string arrays. There can be as many dimensions as you require, provided that there is sufficient free memory to cope with them.

See **array**.

dimension The term is used in describing the size and shape of **arrays**. In number arrays, one dimension – e.g. 'a(1Ø)' – would produce a list; two dimensions – e.g. 'x(12,15)' – a table; three dimensions – e.g. 'q(5,5,1Ø)' – a series of tables, etc. In string arrays, the length of string required must also be given, so that here an array to hold a list of names would actually need two-dimensions: n$(1Ø,2Ø) would store 10 names of up to 20 letters each.

direct addressing (extended address -ing) This transfers data either from memory to a register or from a register to memory.

'LD A,(237FH)' will load the accumulator with the contents of the address 237FH.

All of the register pairs can handle direct addressing, but of the single registers, only A can be used in this way. To transfer a number from memory to any other register, either transfer it *via* the accumulator, e.g.:

```
LD A,(address)
LD C,A
```

or load the pair which includes the register that is wanted – 'LD BC,(address)' – and reset or ignore the unwanted part of the pair.

disassembler A program that translates bytes of **machine code** into understandable **assembly language** instructions. A disassembler is very useful for investigating machine code routines or examining the BASIC **ROM** to show how the Spectrum works.

disk drives The disk drives available for the Spectrum offer a number of important advantages over cassette storage, not the least of which is the speed of transferring data, as files and as programs. A floppy disk is made of a thin layer of magnetic material, protected by a stiff outer cover. The disks can be rotated at very high speeds, constantly bringing a different section to the window where data can be read or written by the drive. This gives rapid access to any file that is stored on the disk. Large disk drives can store many megabytes of data which commercial applications need. The ones designed for use with the Spectrum will typically hold 100 or 200 kilobytes.

displacement A 1-byte number following a relative jump instruction which indicates how far backward or forward the program should branch. In index addressing, the displacement is the number to be added to the index register to give the address of a location.

See **indexed addressing**; **JR**.

display file The area of memory in which the screen is mapped. It occupies the 6144 locations from 16384 to 22527. The way in which the screen is stored can best be seen in this program:

```
10  FOR i = 16384 TO 22527
20  POKE i,15
30  NEXT i
```

This will build up a striped screen as the display file is reset byte by byte. A routine for saving screens in, and recalling them from other areas of memory is given in the entry on **screen dumps**.

DJNZ A Z80 instruction mnemonic. It is extremely useful for program loops. Using the

B register as a loop counter, this instruction subtracts 1 from the B register. If this register does not contain 0 then a relative jump is made, e.g.:

```
        LD      A,0
        LD      B, 12
Label   ADD     A,B
        DJNZ    Label
        RET
```

In this routine, the numbers between 12 and 1 are added to the accumulator.

flag register

Mnem-onic	Operand	Bytes	Clock cycle	S	Z		H		P/O	N	C
DJNZ	displacement	2	8/13*								

* First clock cycle for 'condition not met', the second for 'condition met'.

DRAW A statement (keyword on **W**). It draws a line from the last point plotted (or drawn) to the displacement given. The line can be made to curve by giving a third figure which tells the Spectrum the angle through which the line should arc.

```
PLOT 100,100: DRAW 150,50
```

This draws a line starting at 100, 100 and

ending 150 pixels to the right, 50 pixels up. The x and y values given in DRAW can be positive or negative, but the final point must be within the screen area, as an 'integer out of range' report will result from an attempt to draw off-screen.

```
PLOT 50,50: DRAW 100,0,PI
```

This draws a semicircle, sweeping down, with the endpoint 100 pixels to the right. Negative values will give the opposite sweep to the curve. Interesting patterns can be produced by using values higher than 2*PI (i.e. a full circle). Experimentation with numbers over 400 will give some pleasing results.

edge connector   This is the part of the printed circuit board that is visible at the rear of the Spectrum. Most peripherals will connect to the computer via this board. Each individual connection can be addressed by the central processing unit.

EDIT   (CAPS SHIFT and **1**). 'EDIT' pulls the current line down to the working space at the bottom of the main screen for editing. If a mistake is made during editing and you wish

to reclaim the line to start again, pressing
EDIT a second time will restore the original
line in the workspace.

During editing, the left-right cursor controls (CAPS SHIFT and **5** or **8**) are used to
move within the workspace, and the vertical
controls will not work.

EI A Z80 instruction mnemonic. It enables
maskable **interrupts**.
See **DI**.

flag register

Mnem-onic	Operand	Bytes	Clock cycle	S	Z		H		P/O	N	C
EI		1	4								

element This refers to one part in an array.
The array a(5,6) has a total of 30 (5 * 6)
elements. Each element is identified by **subscripts**. If a two-dimensional array is thought
of as a table, then the element 'a(1,3)' would be
the number in the 3rd row of the 1st column.
In a string array, an element will be a single
character, though normally the smallest part
that is used is a string (which usually has
several elements).

E mode (extended)   Indicated by E cursor. (CAPS SHIFT and SYMBOL SHIFT.) It gives access to the keywords and characters printed in red and green above and below the letter keys on the keyboard. It also gives access to the colour control keys.

ENTER   The most important key on the board: type in what you like, but nothing will happen until ENTER is pressed.

ERASE   A statement (E Mode, SYMBOL SHIFT and **7**). Used in the form:
    ERASE "m";drive number;"filename"
This **microdrive** command erases a file on the cartridge in the specified drive.

error report   an invaluable aid when debugging, and one of the Spectrum's many user-friendly features.
    See **debugging** and Appendix B of the Spectrum manual.

ERR SP   A system variable, address 23613. This 2-byte variable points to an address used by the **error report** routine. As this address can change during the program, it is not enough simply to reset ERR SP. However, the following routine will prevent error reports from being printed, thereby disabling **BREAK**; the code has been placed in the printer **buffer**, but could be relocated:

```
10  FOR i = 23296 TO 23300
20  READ b: POKE i,b: NEXT i
30  LET e = PEEK 23613 + 256 * PEEK
    23614
40  POKE e,0: POKE e+1,91
50  DATA 205,125,27,24,251
```

EX A Z80 instruction mnemonic. It exchanges the contents of registers. 'EX AF,AF'' will exchange the contents of the accumulator and the flag register with the contents of the

						flag register				
Mnemonic	Operand	Bytes	Clock cycle	S	Z		H	P/O	N	C
EX	AF, AF'	1	4							
EX	DE, HL	1	4							
EX	(SP), HL	1	19							
EX	(SP), index register	2	23							
EXX		1	4							

alternate accumulator and flag register. 'EX DE,HL' exchanges the contents of the specified register pairs. 'EXX' exchanges the three register pairs with the three alternate register pairs. 'EX' also acts on the stack 'EX (SP),HL', 'EX (SP), IX' and 'EX (SP),IY'. The flag register is only affected by the 'EX AF,AF'' instruction.

exclusive-OR *See* **XOR**.

EXP A function (E Mode, **X**). The EX-Ponential function, derived from the mathematical constant 'e'. This irrational number (approx. 2.7182818) is the basis of natural logarithms.

'EXP n' is equivalent to 'e^n'.

exponent In the expression 2^4 the exponent is 4 – the number of 2s which must be multiplied together. $2^4 = 2 * 2 * 2 * 2$.

Exponents also occur in **scientific notation** and the meaning is much the same, e.g.:

9.87E2 could be written $9.87 * 10^2$.

9.87E−3 is otherwise $9.87 / 10^3$. (0.00987)

Spectrum will accept numbers written in

this form, and above a certain size (14 digits is the limit), it will only display in scientific notation.

exponent byte Part of the way in which numbers are stored in the Spectrum.

See **floating point binary**.

expression An expression is information given to the computer, usually for evaluation. '2 ∗ 3 + 4' is an arithmetical expression from which Spectrum would calculate the answer. In the line '. . . IF a=∅ THEN . . . .', 'a=∅' is a logical expression and would be equal to 1 if true, or ∅ if not. A string expression might take the form '"Hello "+ n$', and (if n$="Fred") would produce the new string '"Hello Fred"'.

extended addressing *See* **direct addressing**.

false In computer logic, every expression must be either true or false. False expressions are given the value 'logic ∅'; true ones get 'logic 1'.

```
10  LET x=99
```

```
20  PRINT x=99
30  PRINT x=21
```

You can use the values produced by logical operations to operate a simple switch. In a program where you want to flip between two states – changing paper colours, alternating first go's in a game, or suchlike – you might have something like this:

```
IF flag = 0 THEN flag = 1: GO TO . . .
IF flag = 1 THEN flag = 0
```

These two lines can be replaced by the more compact statement:

```
LET flag = (flag = 0)
```

If the flag is 0, then the expression is true, and the flag becomes 'logic 1'. The next time round, the expression will be false and therefore becomes 'logic 0'.

file A collection of data stored in the computer's memory, or externally on tape, disk or microdrive cartridge. Normally, a file-handling program will be used with a number of different files, e.g. with an accounts program you would have different files for each financial year.

The Spectrum offers two ways of saving files on tape. The simplest method is to save the whole program, files included:

SAVE "filename" LINE startline

When the program is LOADed back it will GO TO the given line, and the data entered previously will still be present. Data is only erased by a CLEAR instruction, and while RUN automatically performs a CLEAR, GO TO startline does not.

The second method is to SAVE the file alone using this form:

SAVE "filename" DATA array( )

The name and a set of empty brackets are all that are needed for the array. If the file has a number of arrays, then separate SAVE instructions will be needed for each. Simple variables cannot be saved, though they could be transferred to an array for saving.

filename A file must be given a name if it is to be saved onto tape, cartridge or disk. The filename can be up to 10 characters long.

firmware Hardware is the machinery of the computer – the chips, circuits, wires, keyboard, casing, printers and other peripheral devices. Software is what you write or load in from tape in order to make the hardware do something useful – in other words, the programs. Firmware comes in between: it means the programs that are built into the chips – the routines and data in the **ROM**.

flag In BASIC programming the term 'flag' is sometimes used to refer to a variable that indicates the status of a particular condition, e.g. whether or not the initialization routine has been executed.

flag register The flag or status register is an 8-bit register; 6 bits of it are used as flags and the other two do nothing. They are only changed after the execution of **arithmetic**, **boolean** or **shift** instructions.

bit	7	6	5	4	3	2	1	0
	S	Z		H		P/O	N	C

bits 5 and 3 are not used.

bit 7 Sign flag. It is set to logic 1 if the most significant bit of the result is logic 1 after the execution of any boolean or arithmetic instruction. Using **two's complement** this flag determines whether a byte has a positive or negative value.

bit 6   Zero flag. It is set to 'logic 1' if a zero result occurs after any arithmetic or boolean operation.

bit 4   Half carry. It is set after the execution of a **BCD** arithmetic operation. If bit 4 is set to 'logic 1' after a 'carry out' from bit 3, then the flag is set to 'logic1'.

bit 2   Parity/overflow flag. It has a dual purpose. For boolean, **rotate** and **IN** operations it is a parity flag. If the parity is even then this flag is set to 'logic 1'. For odd parity it is 'logic Ø'. The overflow flag is set after an arithmetic operation when the most significant bit of the result changes from 'logic 1' to zero.

bit 1   Subtraction flag. Used only by the central processing unit when in BCD mode.

bit Ø   Carry flag. After any arithmetic operation, it holds 'carries out' of the most significant bit. Boolean instructions set the carry flag to 'logic $\emptyset$'. It is also used by shift instructions.

Most Z80 mnemonic instruction entries in this dictionary include a table showing how the flag register is affected after the execution of the particular instruction. In these tables, the following symbols are used:

$\boxed{\$}$	depends on the result of the operation
$\boxed{1}$	flag set to logic 1
$\boxed{\emptyset}$	flag set to logic $\emptyset$
$\boxed{P}$	affected by the parity result of the operation
$\boxed{OV}$	affected by the overflow result of the operation
$\boxed{}$	not affected by the operation
$\boxed{?}$	status can not be determined after the operation

FLAGS2 A system variable, address 23658. This can be used to force the keyboard into L or C Mode before an INPUT or an INKEY$ line. Use '8' for C Mode, and '$\emptyset$' for L Mode.

FLASH A statement (E Mode, SYMBOL SHIFT and **V**). 'FLASH' is used in much the same way as 'BRIGHT', and the other 'colours'. 'FLASH ∅' is the normal, steady printing. 'FLASH 1' causes the PAPER and INK colours to alternate rapidly. 'FLASH 8' instructs the Spectrum to print in whichever flash mode is current at the squares in which characters are to appear.

floating point binary The method by which the Spectrum stores numbers. A total of five bytes are used for each number; four bytes hold the digits – these are the mantissa bytes, and the fifth is the exponent byte which stores the position of the decimal point.

The 4 bytes are capable of holding the digits of any integer up to 4294967295 (= $2^{32}-1$), and as the decimal point is held separately, this means that any 9-digit number can be held accurately.

An overflow error will only occur when the number is so large that the exponent byte is unable to cope with it. As the upper limit is 10^{38}

(1000000000000000000000000000000000000000),
this is not likely to happen very often. Numbers below 10^{-38} are treated as zero.

flowchart A planning tool. A good flowchart will show all the routes through a program, indicating clearly the significant events, and the conditions on which branching will occur. With more complex programs, flowcharts should be created at several levels of detail. All of this takes time, but it will generally save far more time later, as a properly planned program is less likely to contain bugs. (*See* **debugging**.)

A variety of symbols are used, of which these are most commonly agreed.

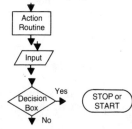

Exits from decision boxes should be labelled, either Yes/No (where the condition is written in the box), or with the relevant variable and value.

FN A function (E Mode, SYMBOL SHIFT and **2**). 'FN name ( )' calls up a function created by a DEF FN statement.

See **DEF FN**.

FOR A statement (keyword on **F**). 'FOR' is only ever used in 'FOR. . .NEXT. . .' loops. The first statement of the loop takes this form:

FOR letter = start TO end STEP size

The 'letter' identifies the control variable, and, unlike simple variable names, this must consist of only one letter. 'Start' and 'end' can be any values, and they set the range through which the loop must run. They can be given as numbers, variables or numeric expressions. ('TO' is a keyword on **F**).

The STEP is optional. It can be omitted if the values are to be worked through in single positive steps, otherwise the step size must be given, e.g.:

```
FOR n = 1 TO 8. . .
```
would take the numbers 1,2,3,4,5,6,7,8
```
FOR i = 4 TO −4 STEP −1. . .
```
gives 4,3,2,1,0,−1,−2,−3,−4
```
FOR j = 0 TO 25 STEP 4.5. . .
```
gives 0,4.5,9,13.5,18,22.5

Notice on the last example that the final STEP is the last one to fall within the given range.

See **loop; NEXT**.

FORMAT A statement (E Mode, SYMBOL SHIFT and **0**).

(1) 'FORMAT "m"; d; "filename"' – this command prepares a blank microdrive cartridge or wipes an old one clear for use by BASIC. The microdrive is placed in drive 'd' and a filename is given to identify the cartridge. The filename will appear at the top of the catalogue. Data is stored on the microdrive tape in sectors. Each sector takes the form of a **header block** and a 2-page data block. The number of sectors on a tape is usually not less than 180.

(2) 'FORMAT "n";x' – this command sets the network station number to 'x'. The network

system allows up to 64 Spectrums to be linked to each other. Each network user must be identified by a unique station number.

(3) 'FORMAT "t";x and FORMAT "b";x' – this command sets the **baud rate** 'x' for the RS232 interface. The baud rates used by the Spectrum are 50,110,300, 600,1200,2400,4800,9600 and 19200. Both 't' (text) and 'b' (binary) files can be sent on this interface.

FRAMES A system variable, address 23672. This is a 3-byte counter which is incremented every time the picture frame is refreshed. As the screen is replotted 50 times a second, this is the rate at which the lowest byte is incremented. The second byte ticks over at approximately 5-second intervals (256/50), and the third byte about once every 21 minutes.

free memory On a 48K machine, with over 40K of RAM available, the question of how much memory is free would scarcely seem to matter, but it can be used up at a surprising rate by some types of programs.

Number arrays, at 5 bytes an element, can absorb alarming amounts of memory. On a 16K machine, the amount of free memory left will need to be monitored more carefully. It can be measured by finding the difference between the addresses held by the system variables STKEND and RAMTOP. Between these two markers are the machine stack and the GO SUB stack, (neither of which usually requires a vast amount of space), and unused memory. Normally, a program will run as long as there are 200 or so bytes between STKEND and RAMTOP.

This line tells you your free space:

```
PRINT (PEEK 23730+256*PEEK 23731)-
(PEEK 23653+256*PEEK 23654)
```

See **RAMTOP; memory-saving; STKEND**.

function   This term covers any type of operation which results in new data, and which usually requires an **argument**. The data may be used directly or assigned to a variable. The form is almost always: 'FUNCTION argument;'

e.g.

```
PRINT CHR$ x
LET z = LEN a$
PLOT COS a*r+x, SIN a*r+y
```

The functions INKEY$, PI and RND require no arguments, and the three screen-based functions, ATTR, POINT and SCREEN$, need two arguments which must be enclosed in brackets 'LET a= ATTR (l,c)'. An argument can be a variable, or an expression which produces a valid result:

```
LET a$= CHR$( CODE n$(1)−32 AND
n$(1)>"Z")
```

This line will capitalize the first letter of a name, if it is in lower case.

G mode (graphics) Indicated by G cursor. CAPS SHIFT and ▉9 takes you in and out of this mode. In it the number keys 1 to 8 will produce the block graphics if CAPS SHIFT is held down.

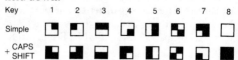

Key	1	2	3	4	5	6	7	8
Simple								
+ CAPS SHIFT								

On the standard Spectrum the cursor controls ([5] to [8]) do not work in G mode (which can make editing graphics lines rather tedious) but on the Spectrum Plus the cursor keys are separate.

In G mode the letter keys "A" to "U" will give capital letters unless **user defined graphics** have been assigned to them.

GO SUB A statement (keyword on [G]). This redirects the program to the line number given after GO SUB, and stores on the GO SUB stack the line and statement number from which it branched.

GO SUB can be used from within a sub-routine, with the return address being stored on top of the one already in the stack, allowing sub-routines to be nested. In practice, the deeper the nesting, the more difficult it is for the programmer to follow the flow of the program, or to debug it.

Every GO SUB must be matched by a RETURN. Failure to do this will result in return addresses being confused, and can sometimes lead to an 'Out of memory' report.

This will happen if a sub-routine is called many times, so that the stack has grown down until it has reached the BASIC memory.

As line numbers can be given as variables, it is possible to write more readable programs, with 'labelled' sub-routines.

```
LET checksum = 2000
. . .

. . .
INPUT answer: GO SUB checksum
2000 REM checksum routine
```

See **sub-routine; RETURN.**

GO TO A statement (keyword on **G**). 'GO TO', like GO SUB, redirects the program to another line, but in this case no record is kept of the branch point. GO TO can also be used as a direct command to start execution from the line given. This preserves the variables that would otherwise be CLEARed by **RUN**. The ability to start and restart a program in this way is another friendly feature of the Spectrum. It enables the programmer to look closely at, and efficiently edit small sections of, the program. Some computers wipe all variables when any alterations are made to the program; others need a RUN to start execution. In both cases, much tedious inputting of data may be required before a routine can be rerun after editing.

graphics   *See* **G mode; high-resolution graphics**.

HALT   A Z80 instruction mnemonic. It stops the central processing unit processing any further instructions until an **interrupt** is sent to it. No flags or registers are affected by this instruction.

flag register

Mnemonic	Operand	Bytes	Clock cycle	S	Z		H		P/O	N	C
HALT		1	4								

hardware   *See* **firmware**.

header block   A file that holds information about a file SAVEd on tape, microdrive cartridge or the network. When a file is SAVEd to tape, a header block is created and is SAVEd just before the file. It holds the file name and type – BASIC or CODE.

hexadecimal (hex) **numbers** These are
numbers in base 16. Hex is more compact than
decimal, requiring only two digits to represent
any number up to 255, and is closely related to
binary:

decimal	hexadecimal	binary
1	01	00000001
2	02	00000010
. . .	. .	. . . .
8	08	00001000
9	09	00001001
10	0A	00001010
11	0B	00001011
12	0C	00001100
13	0D	00001101
14	0E	00001110
15	0F	00001111
16	10	00010000
17	11	00010001
. . .	. .	. . . .
31	1F	00011111
32	20	00100000
. . .	. .	. . . .
128	80	10000000
. . .	. .	. . . .
255	FF	11111111

To convert a binary number to hex, split it in half, and treat each half as a 4-bit binary number. Thus 11000111 gives 1100 (= 12 = C in hex) and 0111 (= 7 in hex and decimal). The number is C7 in hex, or 199 (12 ✳ 16 + 7). The structure of machine code instructions is easier to see in hex. For example, there are clear patterns in the codes which copy data from the registers to the stack:

```
PUSH AF      F5      245
PUSH BC      C5      197
PUSH DE      D5      213
PUSH HL      E5      229
```

Hex numbers are normally identified by a letter H at the end, e.g. FFH.

Decimal/hexadecimal conversion table

hex	0	1	2	3	4	5	6	7	8	9	A	B	C	D	E	F
0	0	1	2	3	4	5	6	7	8	9	10	11	12	13	14	15
1	16	17	18	19	20	21	22	23	24	25	26	27	28	29	30	31
2	32	33	34	35	36	37	38	39	40	41	42	43	44	45	46	47
3	48	49	50	51	52	53	54	55	56	57	58	59	60	61	62	63
4	64	65	66	67	68	69	70	71	72	73	74	75	76	77	78	79
5	80	81	82	83	84	85	86	87	88	89	90	91	92	93	94	95
6	96	97	98	99	100	101	102	103	104	105	106	107	108	109	110	111
7	112	113	114	115	116	117	118	119	120	121	122	123	124	136	126	127
8	128	129	130	131	132	133	134	135	136	137	138	139	140	141	142	143
9	144	145	146	147	148	149	150	151	152	153	164	155	156	157	158	159
A	160	161	162	163	164	165	166	167	168	169	170	171	172	173	174	175

hex	0	1	2	3	4	5	6	7	8	9	A	B	C	D	E	F
B	176	177	178	179	180	181	182	183	184	185	186	187	188	189	190	191
C	192	193	194	195	196	197	198	199	200	201	202	203	204	205	206	207
D	208	209	210	211	212	213	214	215	216	217	218	219	220	221	222	223
E	224	225	226	227	228	229	230	231	232	233	234	235	236	237	238	239
F	240	241	242	243	244	245	246	247	248	249	250	251	252	253	254	255

high-resolution graphics are produced by the PLOT, DRAW and CIRCLE statements. The smallest unit is a '**pixel**', a block of 4 screen dots, and the screen is divided into 176 rows each of 256 pixels. Printed characters and hi-resolution graphics can be used together in the same screen display, and the colour controls, PAPER, INK, BRIGHT, FLASH and OVER, work in the same way as in PRINT lines. Colours can be separate statements, or embedded in the high-resolution statement:

```
INK 7: PLOT 100,50
DRAW PAPER 3;−50,25
```

Colour changes affect the whole of the character square, not just the pixel, so that lines of two different colours cannot be drawn in the same square.

IF A statement (keyword on **U**). 'IF' is only used in conjunction with THEN in the form

'IF condition(s) THEN rest of line'. The conditions are usually expressed as equations:

    IF a=99 THEN. . .
    IF n$= "Fred" THEN. . .

The only exceptions are the short forms:

    IF flag THEN. . .
    IF NOT flag THEN. . .

Several conditions may be tested at once using the logical operators AND and OR, e.g.:

    IF age>12 AND age <20 THEN GOSUB
    teenager. . .

If the conditions are met, the rest of the line is executed. If not, it is ignored, and the program passes on to the next numbered line. As multi-statement lines can be written, it is sometimes possible to write the whole of a branch routine on the IF. . .THEN. . line.

See **condition testing; logical operators**.

IM0 A Z80 instruction mnemonic. It puts the central processing unit into interrupt mode Ø. In IMØ the CPU can execute 8 different interrupt routines – **RSTØ**, RST8, RST10H, RST18H, RST20H, RST28H, RST30H, and RST38H. All 8 are in the first 58 bytes of memory. On the Spectrum this is **ROM** memory and therefore cannot be reprogrammed.

flag register

Mnem-onic	Operand	Bytes	Clock cycle	S	Z		H		P/O	N	C
IM	0	2	8								

IM1 A Z80 instruction mnemonic. It is similar to **IM0** except that it is specific to the RST38H **interrupt** routine. On the Spectrum this interrupt routine scans the keyboard for a key press and is called every 1/50th second.

flag register

Mnem-onic	Operand	Bytes	Clock cycle	S	Z		H		P/O	N	C
IM	1	2	8								

IM2 A Z80 instruction mnemonic. In interrupt mode 2 the central processing unit executes an **interrupt** routine by an indirect call. The 16-bit indirect address of the routine is specified by the interrupt register I (high byte of the address) and the contents of the data bus (low byte of the address). On the Spectrum the

data bus normally holds the value FFH when an IM2 interrupt occurs. Therefore this indirect address can only be placed on the page boundary, e.g. CFFFH, EØFFH.

flag register

Mnemonic	Operand	Bytes	Clock cycle	S	Z		H		P/O	N	C
IM	2	2	8								

immediate addressing In this addressing mode the data loaded into memory or a register follows the operator. For example the instruction 'LD A,3' when executed loads 3 into the accumulator. The instruction 'LD HL,3400' loads the HL register pair with the number 3400.

IN (1) A statement (E Mode, SYMBOL SHIFT and ▆). 'IN' reads signals from an external source (a port), and as far as the processor is concerned the keyboard is external in the same way that the edge connector and sockets are. The keyboard can be read by IN commands (in BASIC and in code). As a means of testing individual keys, IN is slightly quicker than INKEY$, but its main advantage is that it allows several keypresses to be detected at once. Different versions of the Spectrum have keyboards that are mapped in slightly different ways.

(2) A Z80 instruction mnemonic: INputs from the input/output port. 'IN A, (port)' loads the accumulator from the input/output port specified by 'port'. 'IN register, (C)' loads the specified register from the input/output port identified by register 'C'. Used in reading the keyboard.

flag register

Mnem-onic	Operand	Bytes	Clock cycle	S	Z		H		P/O	N	C
IN	A, (port)	2	10								
IN	register, (C)	2	11	$	$		$		OV	0	

INC A Z80 instruction mnemonic. 'INC' adds 1 to the contents of a specified register. If the register holds Ø after this instruction, then the zero flag will be set to logic 1. Otherwise it is set to logic Ø. INC 'register pair' will not affect any of the flags.

See **condition testing**.

flag register

Mnem-onic	Operand	Bytes	Clock cycle	S	Z		H		P/O	N	C
INC	register	1	4	$	$		$		OV	0	
INC	register pair	1	6								
INC	index register	2	10								
INC	(HL)	1	11	$	$		$		OV	0	
INC	(index registers +displacement)	3	23	$	$		$		OV	0	

IND A Z80 instruction mnemonic: INput to memory and then Decrement the HL register pair and the B register. The memory address is held in the HL register pair. The C register holds the input/output port number and the B register can be used as a counter.

flag register

Mnem-onic	Operand	Bytes	Clock cycle	S	Z		H		P/O	N	C
IND		2	16	?	$		?		?	1	

indexed addressing In this addressing mode the index registers ('IX', 'IY') and a displacement number are used to point to a memory address. If the displacement number was 20 and if the index register held 30000 then the memory address will be the sum of 20 and 30000. Therefore 'LD A,(IX+20)' will load the accumulator with the contents of memory location 30020.

See **relative address**.

INDR A Z80 instruction mnemonic: INput to memory and then Decrement the HL register pair and the B register. The memory address is held in the HL register pair. The C register holds the input/output port number. This instruction is like **IND** except that the instruction is Repeated until register B contains Ø.

flag register

Mnem-onic	Operand	Bytes	Clock cycle	S	Z		H		P/O	N	C
INDR		2	21/16*	?	1		?			?	1

* First clock cycle for 'condition not met', the second for 'condition met'.

INI A Z80 instruction mnemonic: INput to memory and then Increment register pair HL and decrement register B. The memory address is held in the HL register pair. The C register holds the input/output port number and the B register can be used as a counter.

flag register

Mnem-onic	Operand	Bytes	Clock cycle	S	Z		H		P/O	N	C
INI		2	16	?	$		?		?		1

INIR A Z80 instruction mnemonic: INput to memory and then Increment register pair HL and decrement register B. The memory address is held in the HL register pair. The C register holds the input/output port number. This instruction is like **INI** except that the instruction is Repeated until register B reaches 0.

flag register

Mnem-onic	Operand	Bytes	Clock cycle	S	Z		H		P/O	N	C
INIR		2	21/16*	?	1		?		?		1

* First clock cycle for 'condition not met', the second for 'condition met'.

initialization In the compiler languages such as PASCAL, and in some earlier forms of BASIC, all variables that will be used in the program must be 'declared' at the very beginning. This is to ensure that space is created for them. In Spectrum BASIC this is not necessary, but establishing variables at the beginning does increase the readability of the program. Even if you introduce your variables as you need them, you will still often need an initialization routine to set up UDGs, read data into arrays, POKE machine code routines into place or take care of any other once-only chores.

Initialization routines are best placed at the end of the program list if they contain large quantities of data or print lines. If located at the top of the program their bulk will tend to slow down running times of the main routines.

INK A statement (E Mode, SYMBOL SHIFT and ⬛). 'INK', followed by a number between 0 and 9, determines the colour of the characters, and of hi-resolution graphics. 0 to 7 give the colours written above the keys, while 8 makes for 'transparent' INK – i.e. it takes the colours already current in the squares where characters are placed. 9 produces contrasting INK. It will be white on the darker PAPER backgrounds (black to magenta), and black on the paler ones (green to white). INK colours can also be changed by hidden colour control characters.

See **INV VIDEO**.

INKEY$ A function (E Mode on **N**). This
reads the keyboard, storing the character of
any key that is pressed. 'INKEY$' can be used
directly:

```
        IF INKEY$="5" THEN. . .   (move left)
        IF INKEY$=CHR$ 13 THEN STOP
                             (ENTER pressed)
   100  IF INKEY$="" THEN GO TO 100
```

Where there are several alternative keys to be
tested, it is safer to transfer the INKEY$ value
to a variable. This avoids problems that may
occur if a second key is pressed during the
execution of the test routine.

```
   100  LET a$=INKEY$: IF a$="" THEN GO TO
        100
   110  IF a$="5" THEN. . .   (move left)
   120  IF a$="8" THEN. . .   (move right)
```

If it is necessary to separate out keystrokes,
then this line will halt program execution
while a key is still being pressed:

```
   90  IF INKEY$<>"" THEN GO TO 90
```

In some programs it may be useful to get the

code of the keystroke, rather than the character. If no key is pressed, then '∅' will be returned, indicating an empty string.

LET z= CODE INKEY$: IF z=0 THEN GO TO.

(start of same line)

See **FLAGS2** for a way of forcing the Spectrum into L or C Mode.

INPUT A statement (keyword on ▮). 'IN-PUT' waits for data to be ENTERed from the keyboard. The statement takes the general form:

INPUT ("input prompt"); variable

If the variable is numeric, then a non-numeric input will crash the program. The input can be a number, a variable or an expression which returns a number.

```
10  PRINT "3 * 4 + 7 = ?"
20  LET answer = 19
30  INPUT reply
40  IF reply = answer THEN PRINT "Good"
```

In this example, the following replies would all be acceptable; '19', 'answer', '3 * 4 + 7'.

String INPUTs are rather more crash-proof, as the Spectrum will accept any charac-

ters as valid material for a string variable. A
safe INPUT routine for a sum would make use
of this, e.g.:

```
1000  INPUT a$: IF a$="" THEN GO TO
      1000
1010  LET flag=0
1020  FOR i=1 TO LEN a$
1030  IF a$(i)<"0" OR a$(i)>"9" THEN LET
      flag=1
1040  NEXT i
1050  IF flag=1 THEN GO TO 1000
1060  LET a= VAL a$
1070  PRINT a
```

This collects the data into a string variable
and checks that only numbers are used before
evaluating the answer. As a further crash-
proofing measure, this form of INPUT can be
used:

```
INPUT LINE a$
```

With simple string INPUT the quotes are
displayed around the flashing cursor. If these
are deleted, either by use of DELETE and the
cursor controls, or by pressing EDIT, then
STOP can be entered. This will produce the
report 'STOP in INPUT'. With INPUT

LINE. . . there are no quotes to be deleted, and STOP will be treated as a simple string. Unfortunately, a LINE INPUT can be crashed by pressing the down arrow (CAPS SHIFT and **6**).

The safest (BASIC) input routine does not use INPUT at all. Instead it takes each keystroke separately through the INKEY$ function, adding each new character to a string until the ENTER key is pressed. A sub-section to the routine copes with deletions. This routine has the advantage that the input data can appear anywhere on the board. If BREAK is disabled, the routine is fully crash-proof.

input prompts These can be written into INPUT lines, and should be included if they will make the program easier to use. Any item which can be used in a PRINT statement can be included in an input prompt, though if variables or punctuation are included, the prompt must be enclosed in brackets.

```
INPUT ("Question value ",qv;" Points. Well,
";n$;"?");a$
INPUT PAPER 6;"Your move :",m$
```

'AT' can be used to control the position of the input, though it will be in the lower screen, where the lines are numbered 0 or 1. If a line number higher than 1 is given, then the input will still appear at the bottom of the screen, but the lower screen area will expand upwards.

instruction *See* **command**.

instruction register It is found in the central processing unit and holds the next instruction to be executed.

INT (1) A function (E Mode on **R**). 'INT' rounds numbers to the next lowest integer. For positive numbers, 'INT 12.345' = 12. For negative numbers, the result is the integer below, e.g. 'INT −12.345' = −13. To round a number to the nearest integer, add .5 before using INT. 'INT (12.345+.5)' is still 12 (the nearest), but 'INT (12.543+.5)' is 13. This works equally well with negative numbers. INT can also be used to restrict the number of decimal places in a number. 'INT (12.34567∗100)/100' gives '12.34'. 'INT

$(9.876*10)/10 = `9.8'$.

(2) An electrical pin on the Z80 micro-processor. Maskable **interrupts** (from the keyboard, for example) are sent to this pin. The microprocessor can be told to ignore this interrupt by software with a DI instruction.

See **DI**; **EI**; **interrupt**.

integer A whole number. For most prog-rammers the word is mainly seen in the 'inte-ger out of range' report that greets an attempt to plot off the screen or access a memory address that does not exist.

interface A piece of hardware that con-nects the Spectrum to the outside world. Strictly speaking, the TV, EAR and MIC sockets and the edge connector are all inter-faces, but the term is more commonly used to mean a separate device. Interface 1 is essential if a **modem**, a **microdrive** or a **printer** (other than the ZX printer) is to be used. Interface 2 is for games players and allows the connection of joysticks and games cartridges.

interpreter The Z80A chip can only

understand **machine code** instructions. To it, BASIC is a foreign language which must be interpreted. The interpreter in the BASIC chip does just that. Each statement in the BASIC program is converted to code before it is executed; a complex process and the reason why BASIC programs are so much slower than machine code ones.

See **compiler**.

Interrupt A signal sent to the central processing unit from a device. On receiving it, the CPU will stop its current task, execute a specified routine and then resume the task it was executing before it was interrupted. Non-maskable interrupts (NMI) are interrupts the CPU cannot ignore. With maskable interrupts (**INT**) the software can decide whether or not to process the interrupt. The Z80 CPU deals with three interrupt modes MODE Ø IMØ, MODE 1 IM1 and MODE 2 IM2.

See **DI**; **EI**.

INVERSE A statement (E Mode, SYMBOL SHIFT and **M**). 'INVERSE 1' reverses PAPER and INK values for any subsequent

PRINTing or PLOTting. 'INVERSE 0' restores the normal state. Unlike BRIGHT and FLASH there is no other acceptable argument. INVERSE 8 will give an error report. When PLOTting, INVERSE 1 will give a pixel PAPER colour but it will not reverse the background colour of the surrounding square.

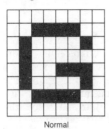

Normal   Inverse

INV VIDEO A colour control (CAPS SHIFT and **4**). This can be used instead of **INVERSE 1** as a way of inverting colours in a PRINT line and the effects are visible in the listing, as well as on the screen. Indeed, INV VIDEO can be used at any point in the list to highlight REMs or other elements.

I/O (input/output) ports These are the parts of the circuit which send signals into and out of the central part of the system.

See **IN; OUT**.

item A **PRINT** item is something which may be included in a PRINT statement – a **string**, number, **variable**, **colour** control, **AT**, **TAB**, **logical** or other expression. The items must be separated by some form of punctuation. Almost any number and length of items may be included, though any PRINT line which occupies more than 4 or 5 screen lines is too long for easy editing, and 22 lines is the absolute maximum.

joystick A moveable stick attached to a base with a fire button. Joysticks are used mainly as an alternative to the keyboard for games control.

JP (jump positive) A Z80 instruction mnemonic. 'JP address' jumps to a specified 16-bit address, which is placed in the program counter. The instruction pointed to by the program counter will be the next instruction to be executed. The JP instruction does not affect the flag register. An indirect jump can also be made: the address to be jumped to can be held in the 'HL', 'IX' or 'IY' registers – 'JR (HL)', 'JR (IX)', 'JR (IY)'. A jump on a condition being met can also be made: 'JP C,address', 'JP NC,address', 'JP M,address', 'JP P,address', 'JP Z,address', 'JP NZ,address', 'JP PE,address' and 'JP PO,address'.

See **condition testing**.

flag register

Mnemonic	Operand	Bytes	Clock cycle	S	Z		H		P/O	N	C
JP	address	3	10								
JP	condition, address	3	10								
JP	(HL)	1	4								
JP	(index register)	2	8								

JR (jump relative) A Z80 instruction mnemonic. This by itself takes the form 'JR displacement'. 'JR 34' in a machine code program will add 34 bytes to the program counter, making the central processing unit execute the instruction 34 bytes after the JR instruction.

The program:

```
JR   2
LD   A,3
RET
```

will jump over the 2-byte 'LD A,3' instruction. The **operand** of a JR instruction is a
single byte. Using **two's complement**, this
byte will be treated by the CPU as a forward
jump if bit 7 is set to logic $\emptyset$ and a backward
jump if bit 7 is set to logic 1 i.e. bytes greater
than 127. JR 252 in a machine code program
will subtract 4 from the program counter and
make the CPU execute the instruction 4 bytes
before the JR instruction. Therefore a JR instruction can only be made to jump-relative
129 bytes forward or 126 bytes backward. A
JR instruction does not affect the flag register.

Mnem-onic	Operand	Bytes	Clock cycle	S	Z		H		P/O	N	C
JR	displacement	2	12								
JR	condition, displacement	2	7/12*								

* First clock cycle for 'condition not met', the second for 'condition met'.

A JR can be made on a condition being met:

'JR C,displacement', 'JR NC,displacement', 'JR NZ,displacement' and 'JR Z,displacement'.

See **condition testing**.

jump In BASIC a jump from one part of the program to another is made either with a GO TO or GO SUB statement. GO TO makes a one way jump, while after a GO SUB, the program will return to the jumping off point when it meets a RETURN. In machine code there are two main types of jump. Assembler instructions beginning '**JP**' produce a **Jump Positive**, and '**JR**' indicates a **Jump Relative**. CALL and RET are used for directing flow to and from subroutines.

keyboard On the standard Spectrum the keys are moulded in a single rubber membrane and bear down on simple press connections. It is a cheap but effective system, and its compact size allows one-handed operation, although it is unsuitable for rapid touch typing. On the Spectrum Plus the keys are larger with a more positive action, and there are additional keys for punctuation, mode changing and cursor control.

keyword A BASIC command word produced by a single keystroke. Keywords are **tokens**.

K mode (keyboard) When the cursor is a flashing **K**, then the next keystroke will be read by the Spectrum as the white word written on the key. The Spectrum automatically goes into K Mode at the beginning of lines, after a colon, and after THEN. Once a keyword has been typed, the cursor will revert to L or C Mode.

LD A Z80 instruction mnemonic. LoaD is the most frequently used instruction. Used for the transfer of data between registers and memory or from one register to another. The load instruction will take different forms, depending upon the addressing mode that is used.

See **addressing**.

LDD A Z80 instruction mnemonic which transfers data from the memory location pointed to by the register pair HL to the memory location pointed to by the register pair DE. It then decrements register pairs HL, BC and DE. For more than one data transfer, the register pair BC can be used as a counter.

LDDR A Z80 instruction mnemonic which transfers data from the memory location pointed to by the register pair HL to the memory location pointed to by the register pair DE. It then decrements register pairs HL, BC and DE. This instruction is like **LDD** except that it is Repeated until BC register pair contains Ø. It is used for the block transfer of data. If the BC register pair contained 100 then data would be transferred from 100 consecutive memory location to another 100 consecutive locations.

LDI A Z80 instruction mnemonic. Transfers data from the memory location pointed to by the register pair HL to the memory location pointed to by the register pair DE. It then increments register pairs HL and DE and decrements register pair BC. For more than one data transfer, the register pair BC can be used as a counter.

LDIR A Z80 instruction mnemonic which transfers data from the memory location pointed to by the register pair HL to the memory location pointed to by the register pair DE. It then increments register pairs HL and DE and decrements register pair BC. This instruction is like **LDI** except that it is Repeated until BC register pair contains $\emptyset$. It is used for the block transfer of data. If the BC register pair contained 100 then data would be transferred from 100 consecutive memory locations to another 100 consecutive locations.

least significant bit Bit $\emptyset$, which can only be worth 1, is the least significant. Bit 7, the most significant, is not just worth most, it is also used in some situations as a flag to indicate negative numbers.

least signficant byte Where numbers greater than 255 need to be POKEd into memory, two, or occasionally three, bytes are used. The number is then stored in the form:

number = 1st byte + 256 * 2nd byte (+ 256 * 256 * 3rd byte)

The first byte is the least significant byte,

worth only its face value.

LEN A function (E Mode on **K**). 'LEN string' returns the number of characters in a string, and is normally used in conjunction with string-slicing operations, e.g.:

    IF LEN a$>10 THEN LET n$=n$(TO 10)

This ensures that any answer has only 10 characters.

    PRINT TAB 16 — LEN n$/2;n$. . .

This prints a string of any length (less than 33) centrally on the screen.

    FOR i=1 TO LEN a$. . .

Here a loop is set up to check each character in a string.

LET A statement (keyword on **L**). 'LET' assigns a value to a variable. It always takes the form 'LET variable = value'. The value can be given as a string, number, variable or expression. In Sinclair BASIC, LET must be used, and it must be a single assignment. The multiple form 'LET a = b = c = $\emptyset$' is not valid.

See **procrustean assignment.**

light pen This is a pen-like device connected to the computer. When the screen is refreshed (every fiftieth of a second) each of the 625 screen rows is scanned and dots of coloured light are plotted to build up the picture. The light pen registers the scan as it passes, and its position on screen can be calculated from the time since the start of that refresh cycle. Light pens are often sold as part of graphic packages which enable the users to 'draw' and 'paint' on the screen. In other programs they are used to select items from a screen display.

LINE   (E Mode, SYMBOL SHIFT and **3**). This word, if used with INPUT, removes the quotes from the input cursor, or with SAVE, makes the program auto-run (at the given line) when loaded.

line   This can be used in two senses – program line, and screen line. A program line is a numbered instruction. Its line number must be a whole number between 1 and 9999. Lines may be up to 22 screen lines long, but editing speeds drop in proportion to the length of the line. Any number of individual statements may be written on a line, as long as they are separated by colons. For character printing, the screen is treated as a grid of 22 lines, with 32 columns in each.

See **AT**.

LIST A statement (keyword on **K**). If no line number is given, LIST displays the program lines, beginning with the first. If the program needs more than one screen, then the '**scroll?**' message will appear. Pressing **N**, space or STOP at this point will give a BREAK message. CONT will not work after this.

LIST followed by a line number will display the program from that line (or the next available one if that line number does not exist). The current line is the first one in the display.

Where scrolling has been allowed, so that the current line is no longer displayed, pressing EDIT will pull back the lines first displayed, and copy the current line into the workspace.

LIST is most often used as a direct command, but can be written into a program.

liveware The people who write software or design hardware.

LLIST A statement (E Mode on **V**). This outputs the program lines to the printer, rather than to the screen, and, like LIST, can start at a specific line.

L mode (letter) Indicated by L cursor. Pressing the letter keys gives lower case characters. For upper case characters, hold down CAPS SHIFT at the same time. To switch from L to C mode, press CAPS LOCK (CAPS SHIFT and **2**).

LN A function (E Mode on **Z**). 'LN' gives the natural logarithm of a number, and is the inverse of EXP, e.g.:
```
LN 3 = 1.0986123
EXP 1.0986123 = 3
```

LOAD A statement (keyword on **J**). In the form 'LOAD ""', it takes the first BASIC program it finds on tape and transfers it into memory. There are a number of variations on this:
```
LOAD "programname"
```

This transfers a named BASIC program to memory. The names of any other programs or data that it finds will be displayed on screen, but otherwise ignored.

LOAD "filename" DATA arrayname () : LOAD "filename" DATA arrayname $()

Here an array will be loaded – '$' indicates a string array. The "filename" does not have to be given, as with programs. DATA can only be loaded into a program where a suitable array exists.

LOAD "filename" CODE start,length

This loads a block of bytes into memory, with the first going to the 'start' address, and a total of 'length' being loaded, any extra being ignored. If 'length' is omitted, then all of the block will (if possible) be loaded. If 'start' is also omitted, then the bytes will be transferred to the same addresses from which they were copied by SAVE. LOAD " " CODE is all that is normally required.

LOAD "filename" SCREEN$

This loads data into the display file, and therefore onto the screen. 'SCREEN$' is identical to 'CODE 16384,6912'.

All types of program, data or code options which are available with LOAD are available with LOAD✳ commands:

'LOAD✳"m";x;"filename"' This loads a BASIC program from the **microdrive**. Both the microdrive number x and the program name must be specified when issuing this command. 'LOAD✳"n";x' This loads a BASIC program from the **network** station x. The station x must be SAVEing a BASIC program over the network for the LOAD command to work. 'LOAD✳"b"' This loads a BASIC program on the **RS232** interface. The **baud rate** must have been set previously with a **FORMAT** command.

location A byte of memory identified by an address.

logarithms *See* **LN**; **EXP**.

logic 0, logic 1 *See* **truth tables**.

logical expressions Take the form 'x compared with y'. The comparison can be any of the symbols '>', '<', '=', '>=', '<='. x and y must be of the same type (numeric or string) but can be variables, expressions or literal data.

logical operators In Sinclair BASIC these are **AND**, **OR** and **NOT**. In assembly language, AND, OR and XOR are used. While AND and OR occur in both languages, and are based on the same principles, they are used in different ways.

logic gate, **logic circuit** The basic units of computer hardware. The most significant ones for the programmer are the AND, OR, XOR and NOT gates. AND, OR and XOR all require two inputs; NOT is a simple 'inverter', changing '∅' to '1' and '1' to '∅'.

AND

C = 1 IF A = 1 AND B = 1

OR

C = 1 IF A = 1 OR B = 1
OR (A = 1 AND B = 1)

XOR

C = 1 IF A = 1 OR B = 1
C = 0 IF A = B

NOT

B = 1 IF A = 0   B = 0 IF A = 1

look-up table Where a routine requires complex (and time-consuming) calculations to be performed, running speeds can be improved by creating a look-up table. The calculations can be done during initialization, or outside the program altogether, and the results stored in an array or as a block of data. Compare these two programs, which produce almost identical screen displays:

```
10 FOR r= 2 TO 30 STEP 2
20 FOR a= 0 TO 2 * PI STEP 2/r
30 LET x= SIN a * r + 128
40 LET y= COS a * r/2 + 88
50 PLOT x,y
60 NEXT a
70 NEXT r
```

```
10 DIM p(96,2)
20 LET n=1
30 FOR a=0 TO 2 * PI STEP .066
40 LET p(n,1)=SIN a
50 LET p(n,2)=COS a/2
60 LET n=n + 1
70 NEXT a
80 PRINT "Start timing now"
```

```
 90  FOR r=2 TO 30 STEP 2
100  FOR a=1 TO 96 STEP 30/r
110  LET x=p(a,1) * r + 128
120  LET y=p(a,2) * r + 88
130  PLOT x,y
140  NEXT a
150  NEXT r
```

The use of look-up tables is even more important in **machine code**, where calculations are more difficult to perform, and the time overheads relatively higher than in BASIC.

loop This is one of the fundamental concepts of programming in any language. It is the fact that computers are able to perform repetitive actions so rapidly that gives them much of their value.

In Sinclair BASIC, loops can be produced in two ways. The simplest method is to send the program flow back to the start of the action routine with a GO TO ... Exit from the routine is managed by a line or lines to test for the required conditions.

```
100  LET x= 0
```

```
110  PRINT x
120  LET x=x+1
130  IF x>20 THEN GO TO 150
140  GO TO 110
```

Sometimes it is more convenient to loop back from the IF. . .THEN line:

```
130  IF x<21 THEN GO TO 110
```

This type of loop is extremely flexible. Where flexibility is not required, the second method can be used. Here the loop repeats the action for a fixed number of times.

```
100  FOR x = 0 TO 20
110  PRINT x
120  NEXT x
```

The result is exactly the same, but the program more compact.

See **FOR**.

lower case letters are the 'small' letters – the characters with codes between 97 and 122. It is sometimes important in a program that the type of letters used in the input should not affect the correctness of the answer. If the required answer is 'a lemon', then 'A LEMON' and 'a Lemon' should be equally acceptable. To include all possible variations in your program could increase its bulk enormously, so the solution must be found elsewhere.

See **CHR$** for methods of checking codes and changing the case of letters.

LPRINT A statement (E Mode on **C**). This behaves in the same way as 'PRINT', except that output is sent to the printer. AT does not work with LPRINT, and neither do any colour controls apart from INVERSE.

machine code Instructions in machine code are executed directly by the central processing unit, unlike BASIC instructions which have to be interpreted first. That is why they are so much faster, but also why programs in code are so much more difficult to write. BASIC is 'user-friendly' – it checks each statement as you enter it to see if it makes some sort of sense, and if your program does have a bug then BASIC will tell you why and where it has crashed. Machine code is completely uncompromising, and unquestioningly obedient. If your code asks for the impossible, the Z80A

will attempt to deliver – and usually lock up in
the process. You will know there is a bug in
your code when the screen suddenly goes
black, or when absolutely nothing happens for
a very long time. Just occasionally, the faulty
code will reach some sort of end and return
you to BASIC.

The first rule in machine code programming
is 'SAVE a copy of your program before you
test it'.

The Spectrum's Z80A chip uses the standard
Z80 instruction set. This consists of over 600
codes, which may be grouped into 4 classes:

(1) Arithmetic – ADD, ADC, SUB, SBC –
addition and subtraction, with and without the
use of the carry flag.

DEC, INC – changing the value of a byte in
a register, DECreasing or INCreasing by 1.

Shifts – SLA,SRA,SRL – which multiply or
divide by 2. If Ø11ØØ11Ø (102) is shifted right it
becomes ØØ11ØØ11 (51); shifted left it becomes
11ØØ11ØØ (204).

Comparisons – CP – are always made with
the byte in A. Flags are set as they are in
subtractions, but the accumulator value is un-

changed.

(2) Moving data – LD, POP, PUSH, EX, IN, OUT – copying bytes from one part of memory to another, or transferring signals to and from the I/O ports.

(3) Jumps – CALL, JP, JR. CALL is the code equivalent of GO SUB. It sends the program to a code sub-routine, perhaps in ROM. JP and JR are jump instructions.

(4) Bit manipulation – RL, RR, RLC, RRC, BIT, RES, SET. RL and RR both rotate the digits in a register. By continued rotation, each digit in turn can be brought to a particular bit, or to the carry flag. BIT tests an individual bit in a register. RES will reset a bit to '∅' and SET sets one to '1'.

AND, OR, XOR – Logical operators are mainly used for bit manipulations, rather than for comparisons.

As well as these main groups, there are other instructions with more individual purposes.

See **accumulator**; **addressing**; **assembler**; **flag**; **register**.

machine code loader Machine code

routines must be POKEd into a safe area of
memory before they can be used. If you are
working with an assembler, then this will take
care of it for you. If not, you will need a loader
program like the one below. It moves RAM-
TOP down to create space above the BASIC
area, then POKEs into memory the bytes it
reads from the DATA lines. The 'address'
must be far enough below the normal RAM-
TOP for the routine to fit comfortably – with
space to spare for corrections and additions.
Here, an 'address' of 65000 (48K) or 32000
(16K) is more than low enough:

```
10  CLEAR address-1: REM use the actual
    number
20  LET a = address
30  READ b: IF b<>999 THEN POKE a,b:
    LET a = a + 1: GO TO 30
40  DATA 62,2,205,1,22,1,16,12,205,217,13,
    62,42,215,201,999
50  REM double check before you add the
    next line
60  RANDOMIZE USR address
```

The following machine code program
should print an asterisk in the centre of the

screen. It uses three ROM routines to direct output to the screen, fix the print position and print the character:

62,2	LD A,2	screen = stream #2
205,1,22	CALL 5633	set stream
1,16,12	LD BC,3088	column and line
205,217,13	CALL 3545	set print position
62,42	LD A,42	CODE "∗"
215	RST 10H	print
201	RET	return to BASIC

mantissa *See* **floating point binary**.

mask Used to read or alter one or more bits in a byte in machine code programs. Many of the computer's facilities such as the colour attributes and system variables are only available by setting (or examining) particular bits in a register to logic 1 or 0, while leaving the rest unchanged. Masks (sometimes called bit masks) employ the logical operators AND and OR. AND allows bits to be read or set to logic 0. If a bit in the number which acts as a mask is logic 0 then the corresponding bit in the number being read is ignored; while if a bit in the mask is logic 1 the value of its correspond-

ing bit is returned. Thus ANDing a number
with 15 gives the value of its bottom 4 bits
since 15 in binary is 00001111. For example:

```
     181  10110101
AND   15  00001111
       5  00000101
```

OR allows particular bits to be set to logic 1.
When a bit in the mask is logic 1 then the
corresponding bit is set to one, whether it is
logic 0 or 1 already. For example, ORing a
number with 136 sets bits 3 and 7 to logic 1 but
leaves the other bits unchanged:

```
     113  01110001
OR   136  10001000
     249  11111001
```

mathematics *See* **arithmetic**; **logarithms**; **priority**; **SQR**; **trigonometry**.

memory There are two types of memory in
the Spectrum – **ROM** (Read Only Memory)
and **RAM** (Random Access Memory). ROM
memory occupies the first 16K of addresses – 0
to 16383 – and consists of the BASIC and the
operating system chip. ROM memory can be

read by a PEEK, but not altered in any way.
RAM memory takes up the higher addresses.
About 8K of RAM is used by the operating
system for the display file, attributes, system
variables and working space. The remainder is
free memory in which your own BASIC or
machine code programs can be stored.

memory saving There are a number of
ways of making BASIC programs more economical in their use of memory, though most
of them either make the program less readable,
or create extra work when programming. The
greatest savings can often be made by careful
organization of the code. There are usually
several ways to tackle a problem, some more
economical than others. If there are several
routines in the program that are the same, or
virtually the same, these should become sub-
routines. The most obvious ways to save
memory are to cut out all unnecessary **REM**s,
and to use multi-statement lines. Each separate
line costs four bytes – two for the line number
and two for its length.

Screen displays can take a lot of space.

Reduce a series of 'PRINT AT. . .' statements to the form:

```
PRINT AT 1,1;"text"; AT 1,24;"more text";
AT 3,3;"even more"; AT. . .
```

This saves one byte for every PRINT that is lost. When simply placing text on an otherwise blank screen, the use of TAB to fix the columns and apostrophes (') to force line spacing is even more economical. The main saving here comes from the fact that fewer numbers are used, and every number takes 6 bytes plus 1 for each digit. A number can be replaced by a **VAL**ued string – VAL "11" is the same as 11 to the computer – this saves three bytes each time. Where there are large quantities of numbers in DATA lines – perhaps for high-resolution graphic displays – memory is consumed at an alarming rate. Store the numbers in string form and evaluate them before use.

```
FOR i= 1 TO 50
READ x$,y$: PLOT VAL x$,VAL y$
NEXT
DATA "100","50",120","50"."135",. . .
```

If the numbers are all between Ø and 255, an

even greater saving can be made by POKEing them directly into memory, deleting the routine which put them there, and simply saving the bytes as **CODE**.

User defined graphics do not need to be defined in the program itself. They can be handled by a loader program, which is then overwritten by the main program. As the UDG's data is stored above RAMTOP it is not affected by NEW, or by LOAD. The data could even be saved as CODE and loaded in at the start of the program. For colour changes, the control characters are far more economical than PAPER and INK statements.

menu This is a selection screen, where the program options are displayed, with a routine to direct the program to the user's choice. Control will normally return to this screen at the end of each section.

MERGE A statement (E Mode, SYMBOL SHIFT and **T**). This will load a program on top of an existing one – without deleting the old program in the way that LOAD would. Any old line that shares a number with a line from the new program will be deleted and replaced.

'MERGE ✱"n";x' and 'MERGE ✱"m";d; "filename"' are the **network** and **microdrive** equivalents of the tape MERGE command. 'x' denotes the station number and 'd' the microdrive number. Programs SAVEd onto a microdrive cartridge using the LINE statement cannot be MERGEd.

microdrive The Sinclair microdrive was designed to overcome the slowness of normal tape operation, yet to be cheaper than disk systems. A microdrive cartridge contains a 20-foot continuous loop of tape, which can be formatted to give structured storage for efficient file-handling.

microprocessor In a Spectrum, the microprocessor is a Z80A chip – a finger-nail sized wafer of silicon that can handle many thousands of bytes of data every second.

mnemonic The word means an aid to memory. The Z80 mnemonics are intended as an aid to human memory. The chip itself is designed to respond to binary codes. When it receives '00111110' it recognises this as 'take the following byte and load it into the accumulator'. Few humans could handle the codes in the same way. They need something to latch on to. In mnemonic form that particular code is 'LD A,number' – a recognisable instruction that could be used for working out programs on paper, and, more importantly, that could be used for thinking about the actions of the chip.

See also **assembly language**.

MODE A system variable, address 23617. It specifies the type of cursor being used.

modem A device which allows a computer to be connected to other computers, of the same or different types, through the normal telephone network. The **RS232** interface, which joins the modem to the machine, converts output to a standard format, so that data, and even programs, can be transmitted or received *via* the modem.

monitor This is a video set, very like a

standard TV set, except that it is specially designed to accept signals from a computer, and therefore can be expected to give a sharper picture. Monitors are either **composite video** in monochrome (usually black and green displays) or colour, or RGB. RGB monitors take separate Red, Green and Blue signals from the computer to produce coloured images.

The Spectrum is intended for use with domestic TVs, although it could be connected to a monitor. This would be worth doing where the Spectrum was being used with a word-processing program that produced a 64 character-column screen.

most significant   *See* **least significant.**

MOVE   A statement (E Mode, SYMBOL SHIFT and **6**). The command takes the form 'MOVE source TO destination'. The source can be either **stream** or **channel** numbers, transferring data from one channel to another. With Interface 1 connected, 'MOVE #1 TO #2' will send data from the keyboard to the top part of the screen. 'MOVE "m";1; "filename" TO #2' will send the program 'filename' on microdrive 1 to the screen. The MOVE command can be used to copy a file from one microdrive to another and send data from one Spectrum to another over a network.

music The sound channel on the Spectrum is not really suitable for serious musical work. Only one 'note' can be played at a time, and there are no ways of altering either the tone or the volume. The quality of the sound can be improved by taking output through an amplifier and a good speaker.

Some independent manufacturers produce add-on units which offer a wider range of musical possibilities.

See **BEEP**.

names given to variables and programs must follow certain rules:

Numeric variables must start with a letter, and may contain any mixture of letters and digits, but not punctuation. 'a', 'age', 'alphabetsortfig2' are all acceptable names. The same variable may be referred to in either upper or lower case – 'AGE', 'age' and 'Age' all mean the same thing to the Spectrum.

Meaningful variable names make a program more readable, but short names take less space, and let routines run slightly faster.

String variables must consist of a single letter followed by the dollar sign ($). Therefore, no program may use more than 26 string variables.

Names of arrays – either string or numeric – must have one letter only, and be followed by $ if they are string arrays.

The control variables in FOR. . .NEXT. . . loops must be single letters only. 'FOR times = 1 TO 10' would not work. 'FOR t= 1 TO 10. . .' would.

Program names (for SAVEing to tape or microdrive) may consist of any combination of letters or digits up to a maximum of 10 characters. To SAVE a program you must give it a name.

NEG A Z80 instruction mnemonic: NEGate the **accumulator**. This instruction subtracts the contents of the accumulator from 0, giving the **two's complement** of the accumulator.

flag register

Mnemonic	Operand	Bytes	Clock cycle	S	Z		H		P/O	N	C
NEG		2	8	$	$		$		OV	1	$

nesting For both the 'FOR. . .NEXT'
loops and the **sub-routines**, the 'Russian
dolls' principle applies. Each unit that fits
within another must be complete and self-
contained, though, unlike the dolls, there can
be more than one unit at any level.

```
10  FOR a=1 TO 4
20  FOR b=1 TO 5                    'a' loop
30  PRINT a,b                       'b' loop
40  NEXT a
50  NEXT b
```

This will not work because the loops are not
nested. The inner loop 'b' must be completed
with a NEXT before the next step of the outer
loop can be taken.

```
10  FOR a=1 TO 3
20  FOR b=10 TO 30 STEP 10
30  PRINT a,b                       'b' loop
40  NEXT b                          'a' loop
50  FOR c= 6 TO 10 STEP 2
```

```
60   PRINT a,c                    'c' loop
70   NEXT c
80   NEXT a
```

Here two loops are nested, at the same level, within one outer loop. The variable b could have been used for both the inner loops.

Nesting is usually essential in programs that handle complex arrays. In the following example the data for the array 'd(5,10,10)' is collected:

```
10   FOR p=1 TO 5
20   FOR r=1 TO 10
30   FOR c=1 TO 10
40   PRINT "Page";p;"Row";r;"Column";c
50   INPUT d(p,r,c)
60   NEXT c
70   NEXT r
80   NEXT p
```

Since control variables in 'FOR. . .NEXT' loops must be single letters, no more than 26 levels of nesting are possible, though in practice any program that attempted to use even half that number would be extremely difficult to follow.

Sub-routines are 'nested' when they are used

within other sub-routines.

See **FOR, NEXT, sub-routines**.

network A network exists when two or more computers are connected together. With the Spectrum this is possible using **Interface 1**, and may be done directly or through modem links. Networked machines can access each other's data, and can all use a single disk drive, printer or other device. Each Spectrum is identified by a station number specified by the **FORMAT** command.

NEW A statement (keyword on **A**). This erases any BASIC program and variables, clears the screen and resets almost all of the system variables. The RAMTOP and UDG limits remain as set so that any machine code or character definitions are not affected by NEW.

NEXT A statement (keyword on **N**). 'NEXT' is only ever used in the closing line of a 'FOR. . .NEXT' loop. When the Spectrum meets a NEXT, it looks up the control variable, adds the STEP to the current value, and checks the new value against the limit set by TO. If it is outside the limit, then the loop is exited.

If you want to leave a loop before it reaches its natural end, then it is best to increase the value of the control variable and go to the NEXT line. Leaping directly out of the loop, and missing NEXT, will build up problems for the future as the Spectrum will continue to treat the loop as active.

```
100  FOR t=1 TO 10
110  IF RND >.5 THEN LET t=10:
     GOTO 130
120  PRINT t
130  NEXT t
140  STOP
```

non-printable characters These are the first 32 in Spectrum's character set. Nearly half of them do nothing, the rest are mainly print controls. For the most part it is easier to use BASIC commands than their control character equivalents. For example, 'PRINT CHR$ 17;CHR$ 6;. . . is the same as 'PRINT PAPER 6'. These characters can be put to good use when reading the keyboard. The following routine would pick up any presses on the 'arrow' keys (with CAPS SHIFT):

```
1000  LET a$= INKEY$
1010  IF a$= CHR$ 8 THEN. . cursor left
1020  IF a$= CHR$ 9 THEN. . cursor right
1030  IF a$= CHR$ 10 THEN. . cursor down
1040  IF a$= CHR$ 11 THEN. . cursor up
```

CODE	CHARACTER
0	} not used
–	
6	
7	PRINT comma
8	cursor left
9	cursor right
10	cursor down
11	cursor up
12	DELETE
13	ENTER
14	indicates number
15	not used
16	INK control
17	PAPER control
18	FLASH control

CODE	CHARACTER
19	BRIGHT control
20	INVERSE control
21	OVER control
22	AT control
23	TAB control
24	
–	} not used
31	

NOP Z80 instruction mnemonic. It performs no operation and does not affect any flags or registers. It is a 1-byte dummy instruction that increments the program counter by 1.

NOT A logical operator (SYMBOL SHIFT and **S**). 'NOT' stands truth on its head. NOT 0 is 1. NOT 1 is 0. NOT can therefore be used, like the other logical operators, in IF. . .THEN lines to test the truth, or falsity of statements, e.g.:

```
10  INPUT x
20  INPUT y
30  IF NOT x=99 THEN PRINT "x is not
    99'
40  IF NOT y<50 THEN PRINT "y is more
```

than or equal to 50'

```
50  IF NOT (x>20 AND y>20) THEN PRINT
    "One is under 21. The second may
    be."
```

Notice how the AND in line 50 works more like an OR, because of the NOT.

A more common use for NOT is in testing for zero values and empty strings, e.g.:

```
LET a$= INKEY$: IF NOT a$ THEN
GOTO. . .
IF NOT flag THEN. . .(flag=0)
```

flag register

Mnemonic	Operand	Bytes	Clock cycle	S	Z		H		P/O	N	C
NOP		1	4								

null string A string variable is 'null' when it is empty. 'LET a$="" ' creates a$ as a null string. The CODE function will return '0' for a null string.

OPEN A statement (E Mode SYMBOL SHIFT and **4**). This command links a **channel** to a **stream**. It has the format 'OPEN#stream,channel'.

operand   Many **machine code** instructions have two parts to them. The first part details the operation to be done, the second part is data for that operation; e.g. LD A,5 (load the accumulator with 5). Here, 'LD A' is the operator, '5' is the operand. An operand could be either data, or an address or a displacement for a jump.

operating system   The Spectrum's operating system is the set of routines in ROM that controls BASIC and the Spectrum's input/output.

operation   An action performed by the computer.

operator   *See* **operand**.

OR   (1) A logical operator (SYMBOL SHIFT and **U**). In BASIC, 'OR' gives the value '1' when statements are compared and either one of them is true, or both of them are true, e.g.:

```
10  LET x=99
20  LET y=21
30  PRINT x=99 OR y=34
```

```
40  PRINT x=100 OR y=21
50  PRINT x=99 OR y=21
```

The number '1' will be printed three times. In an IF. . .THEN line, the statements after THEN will be acted upon when one or both of the conditions are true.

OR can be used, like AND, to test for non-zero variables:

```
IF flag1 OR flag2 THEN
```

OR has the lowest priority of the three logical operators.

(2) A Z80 instruction mnemonic: boolean instruction 'OR register'. Acts on the accumulator and logically ORs the accumulator with data. 'OR A,30' will logically OR the contents of the accumulator with 30. OR is commonly used to alter one or more bits in a byte by

flag register

Mnemonic	Operand	Bytes	Clock cycle	S	Z		H		P/O	N	C
OR	data	2	7	$	$		1		P	0	0
OR	register	1	4	$	$		1		P	0	0
OR	(HL)	1	7	$	$		1		?	0	0
OR	(index registers +displacement)	3	19	$	$		1		?	0	0

providing a **mask**. OR compares the equivalent bits in two numbers. If either or both are equal to logic 1 then it gives logic 1 as a result.

See **truth tables**.

OTDR A Z80 instruction mnemonic: OUTput to the input/output port addressed by register C from the memory location pointed to by register pair HL and then Decrement register pair HL and register B. This instruction is like **OUTD** except that it is Repeated until register B reaches ∅.

flag register

Mnem-onic	Operand	Bytes	Clock cycle	S	Z		H		P/O	N	C
OTDR		2	21/16*	?	1		?		?	1	

* First clock cycle for 'condition not met', the second for 'condition met'.

OTIR A Z80 instruction mnemonic: OUTput to the input/output port addressed by register C from the memory location pointed to by register pair HL and then Increment register pair HL and decrement register B. This instruction is like **OUTI** except that it is Repeated until register B reaches ∅.

OUT (1) A statement (E Mode, SYMBOL SHIFT and **O**). 'OUT' sends a signal to a port. In the following example the port address is 254, and it controls the border colour, speaker and the EAR and MIC sockets. Bits Ø to 2 refer to the border, bit 4 outputs sound. By setting and resetting bit 4, the speaker can be made to buzz. If the border colour is changed each time, then a flickering pattern can be seen.

```
10  OUT 254,1   (0 + BLUE)
20  OUT 254,22  (16 + YELLOW)
30  GO TO 10
```

(2) A Z80 instruction mnemonic: OUTput to input/output port. 'OUT (port),A' OUTputs the contents of the accumulator to the input/output port specified by 'port'. 'OUT (C),register' OUTputs the contents of the specified register to the input/output port identified by register C.

Mnemonic	Operand	Bytes	Clock cycle	S	Z		H		P/O	N	C
OUT	(port), A	2	11								
OUT	(C), register	2	12								

flag register

OUTD A Z80 instruction mnemonic: OUT-put to the input/output port addressed by register C from the memory location pointed to by register pair HL, and then Decrement register pair HL and register B. Register B could be used as a counter for repeated execution of this instruction.

flag register

Mnem-onic	Operand	Bytes	Clock cycle	S	Z		H		P/O	N	C
OUTD		2	16	?	$		?		?	1	

OUTI A Z80 instruction mnemonic: OUT-put to the input/output port addressed by register C from the memory location pointed to by register pair HL and then Increment register pair HL and decrement register B. Register B could be used as a counter for repeated execution of this instruction.

flag register

Mnem-onic	Operand	Bytes	Clock cycle	S	Z		H		P/O	N	C
OUTI		2	16	?	$		?		?	1	

OVER A statement (E Mode, SYMBOL

SHIFT and **N**). In the normal state (OVER
Ø), when a character is printed on top of an
existing one, the old is completely erased.
When the OVER 1 statement has been made,
then new characters merge with any that they
over-print. This will normally make both
unreadable, but is a useful way of creating
interesting images. 'OVER 1' has the same
effect with high-resolution graphics. Where a
line crosses over an existing one, the pixel at
the junction is turned to paper colour.

In both cases, 'OVER 1' works by **XOR**ing
the screen, so that Pixels are only **INK**ed if
only one of the characters or lines has INK at
that point. Where both are INK, the two
cancel each other out.

page 256 bytes of consecutive memory
location. The Spectrum's 64K (65536 bytes) of
memory can be divided into 256 pages. The
first page of memory is addresses Ø to 255, the
second page is addresses 256 to 512, etc. A
page boundary is where one page ends and the
next one starts.

PAPER A statement (E Mode, SYMBOL

SHIFT and **C**). 'PAPER' followed by a number between Ø and 9 fixes the colour of the screen, in the same way that INK controls the character colours.

Blocks of coloured PAPER can be used to create simple backgrounds for games. Images printed PAPER 8 (transparent) can then be moved over the screen without affecting the scenery.

```
10  FOR I=0 TO 21        ⎫ creates
20  FOR p=0 TO 7         ⎬ striped
30  PRINT PAPER P;"(4 spaces)";  ⎭ back-
                          drop
40  NEXT p: NEXT I
50  PAPER 8
60  FOR c=0 TO 30
70  PRINT AT 10,c;" ▲*"
80  PAUSE 10     ┌─────────────┐
                 │note one     │
90  NEXT c       │space here   │
                 └─────────────┘
```

parameter The way in which the Spectrum performs an operation will often depend upon values set in the instructions; e.g. when setting PAPER colours, the parameter is the number given after the PAPER command. In

PRINT AT lines, the parameters are the values for the line and columns.

When linking machine code routines into BASIC programs it is sometimes necessary to pass parameters from one to the other. There are several ways of doing this, of which the easiest is probably to use addresses for data storage. Values can be put into addresses by a POKE, and read by a PEEK, in BASIC, and the same addresses can be accessed from machine code with simple 'LD. . .' instructions. Any locations in the printer buffer can (normally) be safely used for this, otherwise, a space can be left above RAMTOP, but below the start of your code, for the temporary storage of parameters.

parity Describes the state of a register. A register is said to have an even parity if the number of bits set to logic 1 in the register is even. If the number is odd then the register has an odd parity.

PAUSE A statement (keyword on **M**). 'PAUSE (time)' causes the program to wait until either a key is pressed, or until the set time has elapsed. The number after PAUSE relates to the FRAMES counter, and the screen is refreshed 50 times a second. Thus 'PAUSE 5Ø' causes a pause of one second. A timed PAUSE can last between 1/50th of a second (PAUSE 1) and nearly 21 minutes (PAUSE 65535), though any keypress will end it immediately.

PAUSE Ø will make the program wait indefinitely, until a key is pressed.

PAUSEs can be used with INKEY\$ statements to collect keystrokes, e.g.:

```
PAUSE Ø: LET a$= INKEY$
```

This is equivalent to 'LET a\$=INKEY\$: IF a\$=" " THEN GO TO (same line)'.

PEEK A statement (E Mode on **O**). 'PEEK (address)' returns the contents of the address. Any part of the memory can be PEEKed, even ROM memory, where the operating system is stored. Always PEEK **system variables** before altering them and make a note of what they are so that you can restore them in case you decide that the new value you POKE in is not what you want.

Simple number variables, where the numbers will always be integers between Ø and 255, can be replaced by PEEKs and POKEs into a safe part of the memory. The odd unused locations in the system variable area are handy for this – 23681, 23728 and 23729.

peripheral Any piece of hardware that attaches onto the computer in some way is a peripheral device. The list of peripherals available for the Spectrum is long and gets longer all the time – printers, microdrives, disk drives, speech synthesizers, interface 1 and 2, big keyboards, light pens, sound boosters, modems, joysticks, etc. etc.

PI (π) A function (E Mode on **M**). This is one of those rare functions that needs no argument. You can use it as you would use a numeric variable. Because the Spectrum works in **radians**, PI comes into its own when drawing curves, or when working with circles. (2 * PI radians = 360 degrees.) 'DRAW 1ØØ,Ø,PI' produces a curve that sweeps through an arc of 3.14159 radians – a semicircle. The following routine gives a solid

circle:
```
10  FOR a = 0 TO PI * 2 STEP .02
20  PLOT 128,88
30  DRAW SIN a * 80, COS a * 80
40  NEXT a
```
Variations on this routine can be used to create solid segments, perhaps for use in pie-chart displays.

PIP A system variable, address 23609. 'PIP' contains the duration of the click that sounds when a key is pressed. It is normally set to '0', but can be lengthened to produce a more distinct BEEP. In programs for younger users, a longer PIP can give the keyboard a more positive feel.

pixel The smallest element of the screen display that can be controlled by the Spectrum. A pixel actually consists of four dots of light. If each dot were individually mapped, the high-resolution co-ordinates would go up to 352 by 512, and 27K of memory would be needed for the display file.

PLOT A statement (keyword on **Q**).

'PLOT x co-ord.,y co-ord' alters the pixel at the given place on the screen. Normally it will be coloured in the current INK value, but there are variations. 'PLOT INK colour;x,y' will produce an individually coloured pixel. 'PLOT PAPER colour;x,y' will alter the background colour of the character square in which the pixel is plotted. Where 'OVER 1' is current, a 'PLOT' statement will INK in a PAPER coloured pixel, but cause any INKed pixel to revert to PAPER. 'Inverse 1' causes all plotting to be done in the current PAPER colour, deleting any INKed pixels, but otherwise having no visible effect. 'FLASH' and 'BRIGHT' are the same in PLOTting as in PRINTing. Any combination of colour commands can be included in the 'PLOT' statement.

See **co-ordinates**.

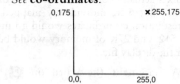

POINT A statement (E Mode, SYMBOL SHIFT and **8**). It is used in reading the screen. 'POINT (x,y)' will give '1' if the pixel specified is INKed, or '∅' if it is PAPER coloured. In a game program, where the screen is used to map the game, POINT can allow more accurate targetting than would be possible with SCREEN$. The following routine uses 'POINT' to produce lines of printing at a right angle to the normal, running upward from the bottom of the screen (useful for labelling the left-hand axis of a graph):

```
 10  INPUT "text?";a$
 20  FOR i = 1 TO LEN a$
 30  PRINT AT 21,0;a$(i)
 40  FOR x = 0 TO 7
 50  FOR y = 0 TO 7
 60  IF POINT (x,y) = 0 THEN GOTO 80
 70  PLOT 8-y, i * 8 + x
 80  NEXT y: NEXT x
 90  NEXT i
100  PRINT AT 21,0;"  "
```

The nested loops (x and y) scan the square in which the letter is printed. Each pixel that is INKed is then copied onto a different part of the screen. The new character can be enlarged by multiplying the figures in line 70, and DRAWing a small block, instead of PLOTting a single pixel. If the multiplication factors, and the block dimensions are made variable, then a very flexible print routine can be produced.

Note that the parameters given after 'POINT' must be enclosed in brackets.

POKE A statement (keyword on **O**). 'POKE' transfers a byte of data into an address, which must be in RAM memory. Any attempt to POKE into the operating system in ROM will be ignored. The form is always 'POKE address,data'.

See **PEEK**.

POP A Z80 mnemonic which transfers data from the stack to a register pair. 'POP HL' would take the first two bytes from the top of the stack and load them into the HL pair. Obviously, it can only do this if data has been placed on the stack by a **PUSH** instruction, e.g.:

```
PUSH HL
PUSH DE
```

```
PUSH  BC
CALL  (ROM routine)
POP   BC
POP   DE
POP   HL
```

'PUSH' and 'POP' are normally used to protect data from corruption by a sub-routine, either in ROM or in your own code. The data is transferred back to the registers by POPping in reverse order. Occasionally, the stack is used as a means of transferring data from one register pair to another:

```
PUSH  BC
PUSH  DE
POP   HL
POP   DE
```

The HL pair now hold the data originally in DE, and DE has been loaded from BC.

flag register

Mnem-onic	Operand	Bytes	Clock cycle	S	Z		H		P/O	N	C
POP	resistor pair	1	10								
POP	index register	2	14								

port Any circuit that links the central processing unit and memory banks with the out-side world. The most important ports are those that connect up to the keyboard and the EAR and MIC sockets. In both BASIC and machine code, ports are controlled by **IN** and **OUT** commands.

power The ZX power supply converts the 240 volts AC mains supply to 9 volt DC for the Spectrum. Any transformer, no matter how efficient always loses a small amount of energy in the form of heat, which is why the power supply gradually warms up. The trans-former will continue to work, and produce heat, even though it is not plugged into the computer.

P-RAMT A system variable, address 23732. This two-byte variable stores the address of the last byte of RAM memory, and will give '65535' on a 48K machine, or '32767' on a 16K machine. If you were writing a program that might be used on either version (but would vary with machines), a check on this variable should be performed at the beginning. It is only actually necessary to check the second byte. 23733 would hold 255 on the larger machine, or 127 on the smaller. The first byte (23732) will always hold 255.

PRINT A statement (keyword on **P**). The basic form 'PRINT expression' has a great many variations. At the simplest it is 'PRINT "message" ', where the message enclosed in quotes is printed exactly as it is written. In the form 'PRINT numerical expression', the expression can be any combination of numbers or number variables that will produce a valid result. 'PRINT 2 + 4 ∗ 6' will print '26'. Where the variable 'n' equals 64, 'PRINT SQR n' gives '8'. Used in this way, the Spectrum performs the functions of a normal calculator.

Unless special conditions are set, the printing will always start at the top of the screen, and each new PRINT statement will display at the beginning of the next line down. This can be changed by using punctuation, AT or TAB.

PRINT lines may also contain PAPER, INK or other colour controls, in any combination and at any part of the line. These commands should normally be followed by semi-colons. The PRINT statement assumes that the display is to be on the main screen, unless output is directed elsewhere. 'PRINT #0. .' and 'PRINT #1. . . .' will make the items appear in the bottom two lines of the screen. 'PRINT #3' redirects the output to the printer, though 'LPRINT' is normally more convenient.

See **punctuation**; **AT**; **TAB**.

printer A peripheral device which produces a paper print-out of the screen and program listings. The Sinclair ZX Printer can be plugged directly onto the edge connector of the Spectrum. It requires no additional interface or power supply. While this is perfectly adequate as a programmer's tool, a better quality printer would normally be needed for serious applications such as word-processing. Here an interface will be needed as well – **Interface** 1 will allow the use of any printer that is RS232-compatible.

The range of printers is enormous, and falls into four main types. Daisywheel printers give typewriter quality lettering, with the best offering a variety of typefaces. Dot matrix printers are an alternative, with the best giving near-letter quality (NLQ) printing. On the cheaper models, the lettering is more obviously composed of dots. A dot-matrix printer can usually copy screen graphics onto paper, while daisywheel printers can only produce characters.

Coloured printing can be done with either an ink jet printer that uses coloured inks, or a ball/point pen plotter.

priority of operations   Where a sequence of operations is to be performed in a numeric expression, rules of priority are followed; e.g. in '1 + 2 * 3', the first operation is '2 * 3', because multiplication has a higher priority than addition. The order in which the expression is evaluated can be changed by the use of brackets, so that in '(1 + 2) * 3' the answer would be '9'.

In mathematical operations, the following priorities hold:
(1) All functions, e.g. SQR, SIN, ABS, etc.
(2) Exponentiation, e.g. 2^3

(3) Unary minus – where the sign indicates a negative number
(4) Multiplication and division
(5) Addition and subtraction

In logical operations, NOT has priority over AND, with OR taken last. Thus in the statement 'IF a = 99 AND b = 21 OR b = 32. . .' the conditions would be satisfied if b = 32 OR if both of the other equations were true. Brackets must be used if the 'OR' is to be tested first: 'IF a = 99 AND (b = 21 OR b = 32). . . .". Now either value of 'b' is acceptable, but 'a' must be 99 if the conditions are to be met.

Where there are complex expressions, any string functions are dealt with first, before mathematical operations, and **logical operators** come last.

processor Normally used as a short-form for **microprocessor**.

procrustean assignment In a simple string assignment ('LET a$ = "answer" '), the variable will be as long as the number of characters in quotes. Where there are arrays,

the length is fixed by the DIM statement. The
array 'a$(5,1∅)' has 5 strings each of 1∅ charac-
ters, so 'LET a$(2) = "answer"' would actual-
ly give the value 'answer ————' to 'a$(2)', and
'LET a$(3) = "the correct answer"' would
make 'a$(3)' equal to 'the correc'. It will be
seen from these examples that arrays must be
made long enough for their data.

Simple string variables can be made to work
like arrayed variables by the use of subscripts.
'LET a$(1 TO 1∅) = "Christopher Col-
umbus"' would chop the name down to
"Christophe", and a short name would be
padded out with spaces to make it ten characters long. This can be put to use in input
routines where the length of the input string is
relevant to the screen display.

The term 'Procrustean' is from the Greek
myth of the robber Procrustes, who made his
'guests' fit his spare bed, either by racking
them or by hacking off their legs. He met his
match in the hero Theseus, who gave him the
Procrustean treatment.

program   An ordered set of instructions to

the computer.

program counter (PC) A 16-bit register in the central processing unit. This register contains the address of the next instruction to be executed.

pseudorandom The numbers generated by the **RND** function are only apparently random. Closer inspection reveals that they follow a sequence. Type in the following program and make a note of the numbers displayed, then NEW it and repeat the process. You will see the same set of numbers. (They have been converted to simple integers for ease of handling. Leave them in their raw state if you prefer.)

```
10  FOR i = 1 TO 10
20  PRINT INT (RND * 10)
30  NEXT i
```

The starting point of the sequence can be made unpredictable by the use of **RANDO-MIZE**.

punctuation The Spectrum recognizes three types of punctuation – comma, semicolon and apostrophe.

A comma (,) after a print item will cause the next item to be printed on the next available half-line.

The semi-colon (;) makes the next printed item appear immediately after the last.

An apostrophe (') pushes the print position to the start of the next line. This may seem a little pointless as a normal PRINT statement will do that, but the apostrophe comes into its own when spacing out items written as a single PRINT line, and for creating line spacings.

PUSH *See* **POP**.

Mnem-onic	Operand	Bytes	Clock cycle	S	Z		H		P/O	N	C
PUSH	register pair	1	11								
PUSH	index register	2	15								

flag register

QWERTY The layout of letter and number keys which follows the standard typewriter keyboard arrangement. QWERTY is the first half of the top row and happens to be pronounceable. The Spectrum has a QWERTY keyboard, though the arrangement of the keys other than letters and numbers is slightly non-standard. The most obvious difference is the presence of extra keys – ENTER and SYMBOL SHIFT (and several others on the Spectrum Plus's board). Trained typists also notice that the punctuation marks are not in the normal cluster at the bottom right.

quote marks Double quotes (SYMBOL SHIFT and **P**) must be used at each end of any literal string, in any situation: 'PRINT "text"; LET a\$ = "answer"; LEN "word".' If you want double quotes to be printed on the screen, then two sets must be written for each set you want to appear.

PRINT """"Hi!"""" he said"

The single quote mark, or **apostrophe** (SYMBOL SHIFT and **7**), can be used freely in printed text, and can also be used as **punctuation**.

radian The Spectrum, like almost all other computers, calculates angles in units of radians, not degrees. A segment of a circle has an angle of one radian when the arc is as long as the radius. This means that a full circle has 2 *

π radians.

  degrees = radians * 180 / PI
  radians = degrees * PI / 180

See **circles**; **trigonometry**.

RAM (Random Access Memory) This type of memory can be both written to and read from. In the Spectrum, RAM starts at 16384. It is volatile and loses all of its data when the power is switched off.

  See **ROM**.

RAMTOP A system variable, address 23730. This 2-byte variable holds the address of the last byte of memory in the area reserved for BASIC. It is normally set at 65367 (48K) or 32599 (16K), with the remaining 168 bytes dedicated to the user defined graphics.

  RAMTOP can be moved up to create more

BASIC memory space by altering the system variable UDG. When protected space is needed for machine code routines then RAM-TOP can be moved down by the CLEAR command. 'CLEAR 65167 (32399 on 16K)' would create room for 200 bytes of code.

random See **pseudorandom**; **RANDO-MIZE**; **RND**.

RAND(OMIZE) A statement (keyword on **T**). This can be used in two quite different ways. In purely BASIC programs it will set the startpoint for the **pseudorandom** number sequence, by passing a value to the system variable **SEED**. IF a fixed SEED value is used, then the 'random' numbers will always appear in the same order, e.g.:

```
10  INPUT "Number between 1 and
       65535 ";n
20  RANDOMIZE n
30  FOR i = 1 TO 5
40  PRINT INT (RND * 10)
50  NEXT i
60  GOTO 10
```

When testing programs it is often useful to

have controlled random numbers, but in a finished program unpredictable numbers are usually wanted. If the form 'RANDOMIZE' or 'RANDOMIZE Ø' is used, then the Spectrum takes the **SEED** value from the **FRAMES** counter, and this is highly unlikely to be the same each time the program is run.

The word can also be used to call machine code routines. 'RANDOMIZE USR address' will direct the program to the code that starts at that address.

RASP A system variable, address 23608. This single byte variable determines the duration of the warning buzz that you will hear when you are writing exceptionally long lines. If, for any reasons, such lines have to be written or edited, then it may be worth while reducing the RASP time. The normal value for RASP is 64.

READ A statement (E Mode on **A**). 'READ variable' takes the next available value from the DATA list, and assigns it to the given variable. Any number of variables can be

READ at the same time, so long as the data is there and is of the right type:

```
10   READ x,y,a$
20   PRINT x,y,a$
30   GOTO 10
40   DATA 1,2,"word",3,4,"next"
50   DATA 5,6,7
```

This gives a 'Nonsense in BASIC' report on the third trip to the READ line, when the Spectrum is asked to assign a number to a string variable. If the last item in the DATA list is enclosed in quotes, then three loops will be completed before the program stops with an 'Out of DATA' report.

Variables can also be READ into other variables. This can save some memory when defining graphics:

```
10   LET I = 255: LET e = 129
20   FOR r = 0 TO 7
30   READ num
40   POKE USR "A" + r,num
50   NEXT r
60   DATA I,e,e,e,e,e,e,I
```

This defines a box into the user defined graphic character 'A'. Only 8 bytes are needed for the letters in the DATA line, rather than the 64 that would be needed for numbers. Even with the memory cost of the LET line, 22 bytes are saved in this example.

recursive A recursive **sub-routine** is one that can call itself. In Sinclair BASIC this is a valid technique, though it would only normally be used where compactness was more important than readability.

register The Z80 central processing unit has 22 accessible registers. The most important registers for arithmetic and boolean operations are the accumulator, B,C,D,E,H and L registers. All are 8-bit registers. The B,C,D,E,H and L registers can be either used individually or as register pairs – BC, DE and HL. Register pairs are useful for 16-bit addressing and arithmetic calculations. The HL register pair is the most important of these. The 7 registers and the flag register F have alternate registers $A', B', C', D', E', F', H'$ and L'. The 16-bit index registers IX and IY are used for index addressing. The 16-bit interrupt and refresh registers are used by the hardware. The stack pointer and the program counter are both 16-bit registers.

A	S	Z		H		P/0	N	C	F
B				C					
D				E					
H				L					

IX	Index register
IY	Index register
SP	Stack pointer
PC	Program counter

I	Interrupt register
R	Refresh register

A′	F′
B′	C′
D′	E′
H′	L′

Alternate registers

register addressing In this mode, data is transferred from one register to another. 'LD A,B' loads data from the B register to the accumulator.

register indirect addressing In this

mode, the memory location to be addressed is held in a 16-bit register. If HL held the number 30000 then 'LD A,(HL)' will load the accumulator with the contents of memory location 30000. 'LD (HL),A' will load the location with the contents of the accumulator.

relation A symbol to express the relationship between two items. '=', '<', '>', '<=', '>=', '<>' are all relations.
   See **condition testing.**

relative jump *See* **JR.**

REM A statement (keyword on **E**). Anything written on a line after a REMark will be ignored by the Spectrum. If REMs are included in a line that contains active statements, they should therefore be at the end.

   REMs do take up memory, and a lot of REMs towards the beginning of the program may slow it down slightly. Occasionally, when testing a program, it is useful to make a line inactive. Insert a REM at the beginning of the line to do this.

REPDEL A system variable, address 23561.

This is a 1-byte variable that controls the duration of the delay before a pressed key starts to repeat. It is normally set to 35 – meaning 35/50ths of a second. In programs for children or other heavy-handed users, increasing the delay time can cut down accidental repeats. If REPDEL is ever put to a very low setting – perhaps in a game, then do include a line that will automatically restore the normal delay. It is almost impossible to type if REPDEL is too short.

reports   The Spectrum is significantly better than most other home computers in the quality of its error reports. They will show you the type of problem that has caused a crash, and the point at which the error affected the computer. The line and statement number given at the end of the report should always be noted carefully. The error is most likely to be there, although it could arise from a mistake earlier on in the program.
   See **debugging**.

REPPER   A system variable, address 23562. This is closely related to **REPDEL**. It fixes the delay between successive repeats of a key, and normally has the value '5' – 1/10th of a second. It can be readily adjusted to the needs of your users and of the program.

RES A Z80 instruction mnemonic: RESet any bit in memory or 8-bit register to logic Ø. It takes the form 'RES n,register' (where n is between Ø and 7). 'RES 5,A' will reset bit 5 in the accumulator to logic Ø. 'RES 6,(HL)' will reset bit 6 in the location pointed to by register pair HL.

flag register

Mnemonic	Operand	Bytes	Clock cycle	S	Z		H		P/O	N	C
RES	bit, register	2	8								
RES	bit, (HL)	2	15								
RES	bit,(index registers + displacement)	4	23								

RESTORE A statement (E Mode on **S**). Each time an item is **READ** from a **DATA** line, the Spectrum's data pointer is moved on to the next item. The pointer can be reset by this statement. 'RESTORE' moves the pointer to the first item in the first DATA line.

'RESTORE line number' moves it to the first
item in the given line. This resetting facility
comes into its own in branching programs
where different branches require different
blocks of data, or in quiz-type programs
where a choice of questions is offered:

```
100   PRINT. . .menu. .
      . . . . . . . . .
200   INPUT "Your choice? 1,2,3 or 4";qc
210   RESTORE 1000 * qc
      . .quiz routine. .
```

Here the data for the four quizzes is arranged
in blocks starting at 1000, 2000, 3000 and 4000.

RET A Z80 instruction **mnemonic** for
RETurn from sub-routine. A RET can be
unconditional, or made on a condition being
true 'RET Z', 'RET NZ', 'RET C', 'RET
NC', 'RET M', 'RET P', 'RET PE' and 'RET
PO'.

flag register

Mnemonic	Operand	Bytes	Clock cycle	S	Z		H		P/O	N	C
RET		1	10								
RET	condition	1	5/11*								

* First clock cycle for 'condition not met', the second for 'condition met'.

See **CALL**; **condition testing**.

RETI A Z80 instruction mnemonic: RETurn from Interrupt. Like RET except that it removes the interrupt request from the input/output port.

See **interrupt**.

flag register

Mnemonic	Operand	Bytes	Clock cycle	S	Z		H		P/O	N	C
RETI		2	14								

RETN A Z80 instruction mnemonic: RETurn from a non-maskable interrupt. Like RET except that it is used at the end of the **non-maskable interrupt** routine.

flag register

Mnemonic	Operand	Bytes	Clock cycle	S	Z		H		P/O	N	C
RETN		2	14								

RETURN A statement (keyword on **Y**). Whenever the program is redirected to a new routine by a GO SUB command, it must be sent back at the end by a RETURN. Failure to do this will leave the return line number on the

GO SUB stack.
    See **GO SUB**.

RGB *See* **monitor**.

RL A Z80 instruction mnemonic: Rotate
Left contents of registers. 'RL register' acts on
8-bit registers (A,B,C,D,E,H and L) or the
contents of a memory location 'RL (HL)'.
Each bit in the register or in memory is moved
one bit to the left. The **most significant** bit is
moved into the carry flag while the content of
the carry flag is a moved into the **least significant** bit.

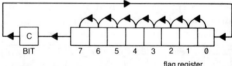

flag register

Mnem-onic	Operand	Bytes	Clock cycle	S	Z		H		P/O	N	C
RL	register	2	8	$	$		0		P	0	$
RL	(HL)	2	15	$	$		0		P	0	$
RL	(index registers + displacement)	4	23	$	$		0		P	0	$
RLA		1	4				0			0	$

RLC A Z80 instruction mnemonic: Rotate
Left Circular contents of registers. 'RLC register' acts on 8-bit registers (A,B,C,D,E,H and
L) or the contents of a memory location 'RLC
(HL)'. Each bit in the register or in memory is
moved one bit to the left. The most significant
bit is moved into the carry flag and the previous value of the carry flag into the least
significant bit.

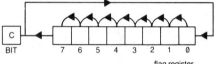

flag register

Mnem-onic	Operand	Bytes	Clock cycle	S	Z		H		P/O	N	C
RLC	register	2	8	$	$		0		P	0	$
RLC	(HL)	2	15	$	$		0		P	0	$
RLC	(index registers +displacement)	4	23	$	$		0		P	0	$
RLCA		1	4				0			0	$

RLD A Z80 instruction mnemonic. Rotate
Left a binary coded Decimal number between
the accumulator and memory location. This

instruction acts on three **BCD** numbers. The first BCD number is held in the accumulator (the bottom four bits of that register). The other two BCDs are stored in a memory location pointed to by the HL register pair. These two BCD numbers are held in one byte, the first in the bottom four bits and the second in the top four bits. RLD will rotate left these three BCD numbers. The BCD number held in the accumulator will be transferred to the bottom four bits of memory. The previous bottom four bits of memory will be transferred to the top four bits of memory. The previous top four bits of memory will be transferred to the bottom four bits of the accumulator.

flag register

Mnem-onic	Operand	Bytes	Clock cycle	S	Z		H		P/O	N	C
RLD		2	18	$	$		0		P	0	

RND A function (E Mode on **T**). One of the few functions that requires no **argument**. 'RND' produces a pseudorandom number between $\emptyset$ and 1 but not including 1. In its raw decimal state, the RND number can be used to make 'choices':

IF RND >.5 THEN . . .

In other situations, it is often necessary to convert the RND decimal to an integer in a set range. The form here is 'INT (RND * range) + startpoint':

LET x = INT (RND * 10) + 10

This gives a value between 10 and 19 – remembering that INT always rounds down.

LET y = INT (RND * 10 + .5) + 10

Now the range is between 10 and 20.

See **INT**; **pseudorandom**.

rogue value A value used to indicate the end of a series of data items. It should be outside the range of possible items. In the machine code loader program, '999' is used as the rogue value. Any negative number, or number over 255 could have been used instead. Where the data items are strings, the rogue value should be instantly recognizable – "XXX" usually serves well.

ROM (Read Only Memory). This type of

memory can only be read and not written to. The ROM holds permanently the BASIC language and the operating system routines. ROM occupies the first 16K of the Spectrum's addressable memory.

The ROM routines can be called up from within machine code programs, and are sometimes the only way to achieve certain results. Because ROM routines are built into the hardware, they are quicker than the same routine would be in software form. The following represent only a small, though very useful, fraction of the total:

703 this returns in the accumulator the character code of any key that is being pressed when the routine is called.

949 the beeper. To use this, HL register pair must contain the frequency of the note (where 0 would be very low), and DE register pair the duration. Duration is not absolute, but varies with the frequency. (*See* **sounds**.)

3438 clears the screen – the code equivalent of CLS.

3545 sets the print position to the column

given in the C register, and the line given in register B. The co-ordinate system is turned on its head for this routine. The lines are numbered 24 to 3 down the screen, and the columns 33 to 2 from left to right.

3582 scrolls the display up one line, while leaving the print position untouched.

5633 sets the stream for output. The stream number is loaded into the accumulator before the routine is called. '2' selects the main screen. (*See* **streams**.)

6696 this will print a 16-bit number as 4 digits. The number must be stored in memory, and its address held in register pair HL. In this single case, the number must be stored high byte first, low byte second.

8020 checks to see if BREAK has been pressed. If it has, the carry flag will not be set. It is set only if BREAK has not been pressed.

8874 given **high-resolution** co-ordinates in BC register pair (y in B, x in C), this returns in register pair HL the address of the byte in the display file in which the point is mapped, and the relevant bit is held in the accumulator.

8933 Plot. Given the y co-ordinate in register B, and the x co-ordinate in register C, this will plot a point.

Many of the above routines corrupt some or all of the registers. For safety, registers should be PUSHed onto the stack before calling a ROM routine, if they contain data which will be needed again later.

rotate *See* **RL**; **RLC**; **RR**; **RRC**; **SLA**; **SRA**; **SRL**.

rounding The conversion of decimal numbers to integers. Where the Spectrum's operating system needs an integer, but might be given a decimal, then numbers are rounded to the nearest integer. This might occur, for example, where PRINT or PLOT positions are the results of random numbers or calculations. The INT function always rounds down.

See **INT**.

routine A section of a program that performs a single operation or a linked set of operations. A routine can contain any number of lines, and major routines may have minor routines within them.

See **sub-routines**.

RR A Z80 instruction mnemonic. Rotate Right contents of registers 'RR register'. Acts on 8-bit registers (A,B,C,D,E,H and L) or the contents of a memory location 'RR (HL)'. Each bit in the register or in memory is moved

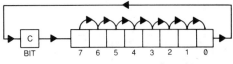

flag register

Mnemonic	Operand	Bytes	Clock cycle	S	Z		H		P/O	N	C
RR	register	2	8	$	$		0		P	0	$
RR	(HL)	2	15	$	$		0		P	0	$
RRA	(index registers + displacement)	4	23	$	$		0		P	0	$
RRA		1	4				0			0	$

one bit to the right. The contents of the carry flag is moved into the significant bit while the least significant bit is moved into the carry flag.

RRC A Z80 instruction mnemonic. Rotate Right contents of registers Circular 'RRC register'. Acts on 8-bit registers (A,B,C,D,E,H and L) or the contents of a memory location 'RRC (HL)'. Each bit in the register or in memory is moved one bit to the right. The least significant bit is moved into the carry flag and into the most significant bit.

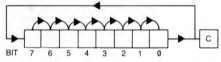

flag register

Mnemonic	Operand	Bytes	Clock cycle	S	Z		H		P/O	N	C
RRC	register	2	8	$	$		0		P	0	$
RRC	(HL)	2	15	$	$		0		P	0	$
RRC	(index registers +displacement)	4	23	$	$		0		P	0	$
RRCA		1	4				0			0	$

RRD A Z80 instruction mnemonic. Rotate Right a binary coded Decimal number between the accumulator and memory location. This instruction acts on three **BCD** numbers. The first BCD number is held in the accumulator (the bottom four bits of that register). The other two BCDs are stored in a memory location pointed to by the HL register pair. These two BCD numbers are held in one byte, the first in the bottom four bits and the second in the top four bits. RRD will rotate right these three BCD numbers. The BCD number held in the accumulator will be transferred to the top four bits of memory. The previous top four bits of memory will be transferred to the bottom four bits of memory. The previous bottom four bits of memory will be transferred to the bottom four bits of the accumulator.

flag register

Mnemonic	Operand	Bytes	Clock cycle	S	Z		H		P/O	N	C
RRD		2	18	$	$		0		P	0	

RST A Z80 instruction mnemonic. Restart RST address. CALLs an interrupt routine specified by the one byte address. There are eight RST instructions and all of them CALL routines in the first page of memory: 'RST ØH', 'RST 8H' 'RST 10H', 'RST 18H', RST 20H', 'RST 28H', 'RST 30H' and 'RST 38H'. In the Spectrum these routines are in ROM and therefore cannot be reprogrammed. 'RST ØH' resets the operating system in the same way as BASIC's 'NEW' except that **RAM-TOP** is reset to its initial value. 'RST 8H' is used by the Spectrum to report BASIC program errors. 'RST 10H' will print the character whose code is held in the accumulator at the time. Before it is used, the output stream should be set for screen. Instructions 'RST 18H' and 'RST 20H' are used by the interpreter. 'RST 28H' is the floating point calculator. 'RST 30H' is a memory management routine. 'RST 38H' scans the keyboard for a key press. This usually occurs every 1/50th of a second.

flag register

Mnem-onic	Operand	Bytes	Clock cycle	S	Z		H		P/O	N	C
RST	data	1	11								

See **interrupt**; **IM0**; **IM1**.

RS232 A serial interface standard. Normally, data is sent on the Spectrum *via* the parallel 8-bit **data bus**. A serial interface converts the parallel data into serial data. The data line is now only 1 wire. To send 1-byte of data requires eleven serial bits. The serial data takes the form of a start bit followed by the 8-data bits – commencing with bit 0. The next bits sent are the **parity** bit and followed by the stop bit.
See **FORMAT**.

RUN (1) A statement (keyword on **R**). 'RUN' starts a program from the first line and performs CLEAR. It also clears the GO SUB stack. As a variation you can use 'RUN line number'. This is identical to 'RUN' except that the program starts at the given line.
(2) After a **NEW** command, if a microdrive drive is present, RUN will search the microdrive cartridge for a BASIC program filenamed 'run'. When found, the file will be LOADed into memory. If the program had been SAVEd

with a LINE command it will RUN automatically.

See **GO TO**; **LINE**.

SAVE A statement (keyword on **S**). It transfers data *via* the MIC socket, saving programs, screens, arrays or blocks of code onto tape. In its simplest form 'SAVE "filename" ' it saves a program, and its variables. As an alternative, 'SAVE "filename" LINE line number', will save the program so that it automatically starts at the given line when loaded. This is useful where you wish to carry variables over to the next use of the program. If the variables are not important, then CLEAR, performed before the SAVE, will reduce the saving time, especially where the program uses large arrays.

Blocks of code can be saved by the statement 'SAVE "filename" CODE first, number'. The address of the first byte, and the number of bytes, must be given in the SAVE, even though they are optional in a LOAD command.

'SAVE "filename" SCREEN$' saves the

data in the display file and attribute memory. Note that the colour attributes of the two bottom lines are also saved.

Arrays can be saved with this form: SAVE name DATA array(), or SAVE name DATA array$(). The array name must be a single letter followed by a pair of empty brackets.

In all of these versions, a name must be given, and may contain up to 10 characters.

All types of program, data or code options which are available with SAVE are available with SAVE✻ commands: 'SAVE ✻"m"; x; "filename". This saves a BASIC program on the **microdrive**. Both the microdrive number x and the program name must be specified when issuing this command. 'SAVE ✻"n";x'. This saves a BASIC program to the **network** station x. (*See* '**LOAD** ✻"n";x'). 'SAVE ✻"b" '. This saves a BASIC program on the **RS232** interface. The **baud rate** must have been set previously with a **FORMAT** command.

See **cassette use**.

SBC A Z80 instruction mnemonic: SuBtract

with Carry. It acts on the accumulator or the HL register pair. 'SBC A,4' will subtract the status of the carry flag and 4 from the accumulator. If the carry flag is set to logic 1 and the accumulator holds 9 then after the execution of 'SBC A,4', the accumulator will hold 4. If the carry flag is set to logic 0 then the result will be 5.

See **condition testing**.

flag register

Mnem-onic	Operand	Bytes	Clock cycle	S	Z		H		P/O	N	C
SBC	A, data	2	7	$	$		$		OV	0	$
SBC	A, register	1	4	$	$		$		OV	0	$
SBC	A, (HL)	1	7	$	$		$		OV	0	$
SBC	A, (index registers +displacement)	3	19	$	$		$		OV	0	$
SBC	HL, register pair	2	15	$	$		0		OV	0	$

SCF A Z80 instruction mnemonic which Sets the Carry Flag in the flag register to logic 1.

flag register

Mnem-onic	Operand	Bytes	Clock cycle	S	Z		H		P/O	N	C
SCF		1	4				0			0	1

scientific notation The Spectrum can display, in full, numbers up to 14 digits long. For very large numbers it uses scientific notation. In this form the number is shown as a decimal with the point after the first digit, followed by 'E' and an integer. The 'E' stands for exponentiation and the integer shows the powers of 10 by which the decimal must be multiplied. '1.23E2' would therefore mean $1.23 \times 10^2 = 123$; '1.23456E15' is equal to $1.23456 \times 1000000000000000$ (= 1234560000000000). Scientific notation can also be used for very small numbers, but if the Spectrum meets any number smaller than 0.0000000000001 it treats it as zero.

SCRCT A system variable, address 23692. Normally, when the print position reaches the bottom of the screen, you will see the '**scroll?**' message. If you wish to create an automatic scroll it can be done by altering SCRCT (SCRoll CounT). Set it to be one more than the number of lines that you want to scroll, or keep resetting it with a high number (up to 255) to get continuous scrolling. Then set to

'1' to restore normal operation, e.g.:

```
10  LET number = 0
20  POKE 23692,10
30  PRINT number
40  LET number = number + 1
50  GOTO 30
```

Try this with different values in line 20, and also see the effect of replacing the last line with 'GO TO 20'.

screen The screen uses different co-ordinate sets but a single memory map for PRINTing and PLOTting. This makes it difficult to POKE characters or graphics directly on to the screen.

See **PRINT**; **PLOT**; **display file**.

screen dump Complex screens take a while to create. Even simple printed screens take a few seconds. Sometimes you may want to have an alternative screen display instantly. This can be achieved with a remarkably simple machine code routine. At the heart of it is the compound instruction 'LDIR' (Load, Decrement, Increment and Repeat). It works on the three register pairs BC, DE and HL. Load the address in DE from the address in HL; Decrement BC; Increment DE and HL. This continues until BC is zero. Using LDIR, data can be copied from the screen and attributes memory areas into a protected area above RAMTOP, then back down again later when required.

```
LD BC,6144  (length of screen memory)
LD HL,16384 (start of screen memory)
LD DE,??    dump address
LDIR
```

As the screen takes over 6K of memory, with another 768 bytes required for the attributes, the dump must be as big. The 16K machine has only room for a single dump. On a 48K machine, there is room for 5 full screen dumps (so long as the accompanying program is short).

Here the dump is located at 25344, and the routine fits in just below it:

```
10  CLEAR 25319
20  LET a = 25320
30  READ b: IF b<>999 THEN POKE a,b:
    LET a = a + 1: GO TO 30
40  DATA 1,0,27,33,0,64,17,0,99,237,176,201
```

```
 50  REM screen to dump
 60  DATA
     1,0,27,33,0,99,17,0,64,237,176,201,999
 70  REM dump to screen
 80  ... lines to create screen
  . .
200  RANDOMIZE USR 25320: REM screen
     to dump
210  CLS: PAUSE 0
220  RANDOMIZE USR 25332: REM recall
     screen
```

See **machine code; display file**.

SCREEN$ A function. (E Mode, SYM-
BOL SHIFT and **K**). This is used for reading
the screen. 'SCREEN$ (line, column)' will
return the character, if any, at the given place.
Unfortunately, SCREEN$ cannot recognize
any graphics, which restricts its value to games
programmers. The line and column figures
must always be enclosed in brackets.

See **SAVE**, for another use of SCREEN$.

scroll? This message will appear during
PRINTing or LISTing, if the Spectrum has
more than 22 lines of material to display on the

screen. Pressing any key, apart from **N**, space, BREAK, or STOP, will cause the printing to scroll (roll upwards one line at a time) until the screen is filled with new lines, or until there are no more to display.

See **SCRCT**.

SEED A system variable, address 23670. This 2-byte variable sets the startpoint for the **pseudorandom** number sequence. The seed number can be POKEd in here, but it is simpler to use the form 'RANDOMIZE number', which has exactly the same effect.

semi-colon Punctuation (SYMBOL SHIFT and **O**). A semi-colon (;) placed after an item in a PRINT line will make the next item appear directly after the last:

```
10  FOR n = 65 TO 90
20  PRINT n;CHR$ n;
30  NEXT n
40  PRINT "END"
```

Semi-colons should be used where the PRINT items are colour changes or AT instructions:

```
. . .  PRINT AT 4,1; PAPER 6; INK 0;
```

"left"; AT 4,25; BRIGHT 1; "right"

See **punctuation**.

serial   Sending bits down a single wire as a series of positive and negative charges. In parallel transmission, the bits travel simultaneously down a set of 8 wires, with logic 1s signified by positive charges, and logic Øs shown by the absence of charge.

See **RS232**.

SET   A Z80 instruction mnemonic which SETs any bit in memory or 8-bit register to logic 1. It takes the form 'SET n,register', where n is between Ø and 7. 'SET 7,A' will set the bit 7 in the accumulator to logic 1. 'SET 6,(HL)' will set the bit 5 in memory (pointed to by register pair HL) to logic 1.

flag register

Mnem-onic	Operand	Bytes	Clock cycle	S	Z		H		P/O	N	C
SET	bit, register	2	8								
SET	bit, (HL)	2	15								
SET	bit,($\begin{smallmatrix}\text{index registers}\\ +\text{displacement}\end{smallmatrix}$)	4	23								

SGN   A function (E Mode on **H**). 'SGN

number' will give −1 if the number is negative, Ø if zero or 1 if positive. The number is not affected by the function. It could prove of use in situations where a three-way branch exists, and the direction is conditional upon whether a number is negative, positive or zero: '. . .GO TO 1ØØØ + 1ØØ   SGN x. . .'; or 'LET line = line + SGN x. . .'. The actual size of the number is irrelevant to the SGN function.

SIN   A function (E Mode on). Given an angle, in radians, this returns the sine.

See **circle**; **trigonometry**.

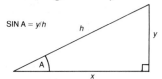

SIN A = y/h

SLA   A Z80 instruction mnemonic: Shift Left Arithmetic contents of register. Acts on 8-bit registers (A,B,C,D,E,H and L) or the contents of a memory location 'SLA (HL)'. Each bit in the register or in memory is moved one bit to the left. The most significant bit is moved into the carry flag and the least significant bit is set to logic Ø. Used for multiplying the register or memory by 2.

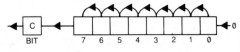

flag register

Mnemonic	Operand	Bytes	Clock cycle	S	Z		H		P/O	N	C
SLA	register	2	8	$	$		Ø		P	Ø	$
SLA	(HL)	2	15	$	$		Ø		P	Ø	$
SLA	(index registers +displacement)	4	23	$	$		Ø		P	Ø	$

slice *See* **string slicing**.

software *See* **firmware**.

sort The following program demonstrates an alternative to **bubble sorting** as a way of ordering lists. It works by reordering the set from the top down. On each pass through the list, it finds the biggest number and swaps that with the one at the top of the list. Each pass begins one number further down the list, and

with large sets this can make it faster than a
bubble sort, where each pass goes through the
full list.

```
 10  DIM n(50)
 20  FOR i = 1 TO 50
 30  LET n(i) = INT (RND * 100)
 40  NEXT i
 50  REM get 50 random numbers
 60  FOR j = 1 TO 49
 70  LET biggest = 0
 80  FOR k = j TO 50
 90  IF n(k) > biggest THEN LET biggest
      = n(k): LET swap = k
100  NEXT k
110  LET spare = n(j): LET n(j) =
      n(swap): LET n(swap) = spare
120  PRINT n(j)
130  NEXT j
```

sounds These can be produced by the
BEEP statement through the built-in speaker.
The beeper can also be called up by simple
machine code routines. To make it work, the
HL register pair must be loaded with the
frequency of the note, and the DE pair with

the duration. In practice, the actual length of the note depends upon both values; a given 'duration' will produce longer notes at low than at high frequencies.

Here the note will keep sounding until the BREAK/SPACE key is pressed:

```
LD    HL,frequency
LD    DE,duration
CALL  BEEPER   (03B5H = 181,3)
CALL  GETKEY   (02BFH = 191,2)
CP    32       Check for 32 — space CODE
RET   Z        Return if space pressed
JR    start
```

In this example the frequency is set to 1638 (102,6) — 'C', and the duration to 16:

```
10  CLEAR 32499
20  LET a = 32500
30  READ b: IF b<>999 THEN POKE a,b:
    LET a = a + 1: GO TO 30
40  DATA 33,102,6,17,16,0,205,181,3
50  DATA 205,191,2,254,32,200,24,239,999
60  RANDOMIZE USR 32500
```

speech synthesizer Most speech synthesizers work by storing a wide range of possible sounds, or allophones, which can be combined into words. In some devices, special control characters are used to determine which sound a letter should make. Others use only normal spelling, and select the appropriate allophone by examining the context of the letter.

SQR　A function (E Mode on). 'SQR number' returns the square root of a number. This could be replaced by the form 'number $\uparrow$ (1/2)' (which represents 'number $^{(\frac{1}{2})}$')

SQR 64 = 64 $\uparrow$ (1/2) = 8

To find cube and other roots, use variations on the second square root method. '27 $\uparrow$ (1/3)' gives the cube root of 27. '256 $\uparrow$ (1/8)' finds the eighth root of 256.

square of a number　This can be found using the exponentiation sign ($\uparrow$ – SYMBOL SHIFT and), or by multiplying by itself: '2 $\uparrow$ 2' = 2 $*$ 2. Higher powers of numbers can be found in the same way: '5 $\uparrow$ 4' = 5 $*$ 5 $*$ 5 $*$ 5.

SRA　A Z80 instruction mnemonic: Shift

Right Arithmetic contents of register. It acts on 8-bit registers (A,B,C,D,E,H and L) or the contents of a memory location 'SRA (HL)'. Each bit in the register or in memory is moved one bit to the right, except for the most significant bit. The **least significant bit** is moved into the carry flag and bit 6 is set to logic Ø. Because bit 7 is not changed, the sign of the byte is not changed (**two's complement**). SRA is used for dividing the register or memory by 2 and at the same time preserving the sign of the data.

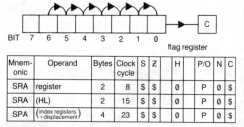

flag register

Mnem-onic	Operand	Bytes	Clock cycle	S	Z		H		P/O	N	C
SRA	register	2	8	$	$		Ø		P	Ø	$
SRA	(HL)	2	15	$	$		Ø		P	Ø	$
SPA	(index registers +displacement)	4	23	$	$		Ø		P	Ø	$

SRL A Z80 instruction mnemonic: Shift Right Logical contents of register. It acts on 8-bit registers (A,B,C,D,E,H and L) or the contents of a memory location 'SRL (HL)'. Each bit in the register or in memory is moved one bit to the right. The **least significant bit** is moved into the carry flag and the most significant bit is set to logic $\emptyset$. SRL is used for dividing the register or memory by 2.

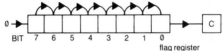

Mnemonic	Operand	Bytes	Clock cycle	S	Z		H		P/O	N	C
SRL	register	2	8	$	$		$\emptyset$		P	$\emptyset$	$
SRL	(HL)	2	15	$	$		$\emptyset$		P	$\emptyset$	$
SRL	(index registers +displacement)	4	23	$	$		$\emptyset$		P	$\emptyset$	$

stack (1) An area of memory used by the computer for the temporary storage of data. BASIC uses a stack for its GO SUB statement. The Z80 central processing unit also has a stack.

(2) In this addressing mode the stack is used for data storage. **PUSH** and **POP** are examples of this form of addressing.

See **stack pointer**.

stack pointer (SP) A 16-bit Z80 register which points to the next free memory address at which data can be stored. The last byte to be placed on to the stack is the first byte taken off. Each time a single byte is stored on the stack the stack pointer is decremented (moves down in memory) by 1.

　See **PUSH**; **POP**.

statement In Sinclair BASIC, 'statement' can mean a BASIC command word, such as PRINT, BEEP, GO TO. It can also mean the word used (normally with arguments) in a program line, e.g. 'PRINT "hello" ', 'BEEP 1,—1Ø.

status register Another term for **flag register**.

STEP A statement. (SYMBOL SHIFT and **D**). 'STEP' is used in FOR. . .TO. . . lines to set the value by which the control variable is incremented on each pass through the loop. Where the increment is +1, the STEP can be omitted.

　See **FOR**.

STKEND   A system variable, address 23653. (This 2-byte variable must not be POKEd). It contains the address of the start of free space, and can be used with RAMTOP to find the amount of memory left.

See **free memory**.

STOP   A statement (SYMBOL SHIFT and **A**). 'STOP' halts program execution, although it can be restarted by CONT. During the **debugging** phase of programming it is sometimes useful to insert temporary STOP lines so that routines can be examined with care.

store   Any medium into which data can be transferred from the central processing unit, to be retained for future use. **RAM**, tape, disk and **microdrive** cartridge are all storage media.

**STR$**   A function (E Mode on **Y**). This converts a number into a string. 'STR$ 99' is "99". It might be used with other functions to produce a controlled screen display:

    PRINT TAB 32— LEN STR$ answer. . .

This would print the answer, whatever its size, so that the last digit was in the rightmost column of the screen.

stream The route taken by data between **channels**. There are 16 streams on the Spectrum numbered #0 to #15. Four of these streams (#0 to #3) are already defined on the Spectrum, and the rest can be programmed by the user. Streams #0 and #1 can output data to the lower part of the main screen and input data from the keyboard. Stream #2 outputs data to the screen but cannot be input, being a one-way stream. Stream #3 outputs data to the printer but cannot input.

string A set of characters. The length of the string depends entirely on the programmer – there are no fixed upper limits on the Spectrum, unlike most other home computers. The only restriction is the amount of free memory available. A string can have no characters at all – it is then called a **null string**.

Any literal strings must be enclosed in double quotes, e.g. "text for printing". String variables are signified by the dollar sign ($).

See **array**; **substring**; **variable**.

string concatenation Joining strings
together. This is done using the addition sign
'+':
```
10   LET a$ = "string"
20   LET b$ = "word"
30   LET c$ = a$ + b$
40   LET d$ = a$ + " " + "text"
50   PRINT c$,d$
```
This will display 'stringword' and 'string
text'. The same string can be joined to itself:
```
10   LET a$ = "*"
20   LET a$ = a$ + a$
30   PRINT a$
40   LET a$ = a$ + a$ + a$ + a$
50   PRINT a$
```

string slicing This is done using the operator 'TO'. 'a$(2 TO 5)' refers to those charac-
ters between and including the second and the
fifth in the string.
```
10   LET a$ = "testing"
20   PRINT a$(3 TO 5)
30   LET b$ = a$(1 TO 4)
40   PRINT b$: LET c$ = b$ + "piece"
```

```
50  PRINT c$(1 TO 8)
```

This will print 'tin', 'test' and 'testpiec'. Notice that when characters are assigned to a string of a set size, then any extra characters are ignored (*See* **procrustean assignment**). Where the slice takes in the first, or last, characters of a string, the end subscripts can be omitted. 'a$(TO 5)' is the same as 'a$(1 TO 5)'; 'a$(8 TO)' is the same as 'a$(8 TO LEN a$)'.

structured programming All programs have a structure, but sometimes it is not very clear. To earn the label 'structured', a program must have a crisp, logical framework, with each section written as a self-contained routine or sub-routine. These will have been tested independently before being incorporated in the main program. The shape of the program will have been decided at the flowchart stage.

Some argue that structured programs can only be written where there are procedures – routines which can be called up by name, and which perform specific functions. Sinclair BASIC has no procedures, but sub-routines can work in much the same way.

See **GO SUB**.

SUB A Z80 instruction mnemonic. SUB can only be used for 8-bit arithmetic, and always acts on the accumulator. The number to be subtracted can be given directly ('SUB n'), held in a register ('SUB B', 'SUB H'), or in memory ('SUB (HL)', 'SUB (IX+n)'). Unlike SBC, the contents of the carry flag are ignored when the subtraction takes place, although the flag is affected by the result.

For 16-bit subtraction, the SBC instruction must be used.

See **condition testing**.

flag register

Mnem-onic	Operand	Bytes	Clock cycle	S	Z		H		P/O	N	C
SUB	data	2	7	$	$		$		OV	1	$
SUB	register	1	4	$	$		$		OV	1	$
SUB	(HL)	1	7	$	$		$		OV	1	$
SUB	(index registers +displacement)	3	19	$	$		$		OV	1	$

sub-routine A section of a program that is accessed by a GO SUB command, and which

ends with RETURN. Sub-routines can be
used from within other sub-routines.

See **nesting**; **GO SUB**.

subscript The reference numbers in substrings and subscripted (arrayed) variables.
Subscripts are always enclosed by brackets.
The lowest subscript possible in either an array
or a string is '1'.

substring The section of a string that is
produced by slicing. A substring can consist of
one character, e.g. 'a$(4)'; or a group – 'a$(3
TO 9)'.

symbol The Spectrum character set can be
divided into symbols (single characters) and
tokens (words). In a narrower sense, symbol
also means a mathematical or other sign, hence
SYMBOL SHIFT. Many of the characters
obtained when this key is held down are
symbols.

syntax error BASIC, like all languages,
has its own syntax or grammatical structure. If
you try to enter a line which fails to make
sense in BASIC, the Spectrum recognizes the

syntax error and indicates it with a flashing ❓ cursor. This refusal to accept incorrect instructions is one of the exceptional features of the Spectrum. Most computers accept anything, and only tell you of your error when they try to execute the line.

system variable The block of memory between 23552 and 23733 is occupied by a set of variables needed by the operating system. Some of these can be safely altered by a programmer to produce particular effects. Others should never be POKEd as the data held there is crucial to the system. PEEKing the variables is always possible, and can throw interesting lights on how the system works.

See **BORDCR; CHARS; DF SZ; ERR SP; FRAMES; MODE; PIP; P—RAMT; RAMTOP; RASP; REPDEL; REPPER; SCRCT; SEED; STKEND; UDG.**

TAB A **PRINT** operator (E Mode on **P**). 'TAB' sets the column at which the next print item will start to appear. This will be on the same line if the TAB column is to the right of the current print position, but otherwise on the next line down, e.g.:

```
PRINT "start"; TAB 13;"middle"; TAB
28;"end"; TAB 4;"next line"
```

TAB is frequently used for displaying tables:

```
10 FOR i = 1 TO 10
20 PRINT TAB 4;i; TAB 14;i * 2; TAB
   24;i * 3
30 NEXT i
```

TAN A function (E Mode on **E**). Given an angle in radians, 'TAN' returns the tangent.
See **trigonometry**.

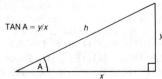

TAN A = y/x

THEN A statement (SYMBOL SHIFT and **G**). 'THEN' is only ever used as part of an IF. . .THEN line.
See **IF**; **condition testing**.

TO An operator (SYMBOL SHIFT and **F**).

'TO' is used in the FOR. . . statement and in
substrings. 'FOR i = 1 TO 100. . .' sets the
start and end limits for the loop. In substrings,
'TO' again sets the range – 'a$(3 TO 9)' slices
off all characters from the 3rd to the 9th
inclusive.

token A character code which calls up a
BASIC word or a compound symbol rather
than a single character. All of the characters
with CODEs above 164 are tokens, and all are
keywords, apart from 199, 200 and 201 which
are the symbols '<=', '>=' and '<>'.

trigonometry The Spectrum uses **radians**
as units when working on the trigonometrical
functions SIN, COS, TAN, ASN, ACS and
ATN.

In the triangle ABC:
SIN a = BC/AC = opposite/hypotenuse
COS a= AB/AC = adjacent/hypotenuse
TAN a= BC/AB = opposite/adjacent

When plotting a circle using the trigonometrical functions:

x = x co-ord. of centre + COS a $*$ radius
y = y co-ord. of centre + SIN a $*$ radius

This is demonstrated in the following program (notice where the circle starts):

```
10 FOR a = 0 TO 2 * PI STEP .02
20 LET c = COS a
30 LET s = SIN a
40 PRINT AT 0,0;c,s
50 LET x = 128 + c * 80
60 LET y = 88 + s * 80
70 PLOT x,y
80 PAUSE 0
90 NEXT a
```

If 'c' and 's' are exchanged, the circle will start from the top and be drawn clockwise.

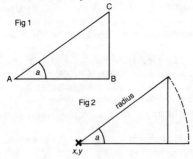

Fig 1

Fig 2

radius

Where the Sine, Cosine or Tangent of an angle is known, the angle can be found by using the appropriate Arc-function: Arcsine (ASN), Arccosine (ASC) or Arctangent (ATN).

See **radian**; **circle**.

true   Where Spectrum logic is concerned, a true statement has a value of 1, e.g.:

```
10 LET a = 99
20 PRINT (a = 99)
30 PRINT (2 + 2 = 4)
```

Any statement written in brackets will be evaluated in terms of truth.

See **false**; **logical operators**.

TRUE VIDEO   (CAPS SHIFT and **3**). This restores the normal display, with characters being printed in INK colour on PAPER coloured background. The control works within the program list as well as in screen displays.

See **INVERSE VIDEO**.

truth tables   These are a convenient way of displaying the results of logical operations. With operators that compare two inputs, there will be four possible outputs. Here, inputs and outputs are expressed in terms of logic 1s and logic Øs, but they could be called Trues and Falses instead:

AND			OR			XOR		
x	y	x AND y	x	y	x OR y	x	y	x XOR y
0	0	0	0	0	0	0	0	0
1	0	0	1	0	1	1	0	1
0	1	0	0	1	1	0	1	1
1	1	1	1	1	1	1	1	0

(x AND y) is true only where both x and y are true. (x OR y) is true if either or both are true. (x XOR y) is true only if one is true, but not if both are.

two's complement (TC) A way of taking away by adding, using the complements of numbers. In the decimal system, the complement of a number is the number which must be added to it to make 9 – the complement of 6 is 3. '7 − 6' is the same as '7 + 3 − 9'. This is not very helpful, but if 1 is added to the complement, the sum becomes very simple – '7 + 4 − 10'.

In 8-bit binary, the two's complement is the number which must be added to make 255.

This can be found very simply by changing all
1s to Ø, and all Øs to 1, and then adding 1. The
two's complement of 1Ø1Ø1Ø1Ø (170) is
Ø1Ø1Ø11Ø (86). Following the earlier, decimal
example, you would expect to have to deduct
256 from the addition, but in practice this is
not necessary, as the 8-bit number cannot hold
the overflow, e.g.:

```
  125    Ø1111101
-  78    Ø1001110   TC = 10110001+1 = 178
=  47
```

```
  125    Ø1111101
+178    10110010
=303    100101110
-256    100000000
=  47    00101110
```

Two's complement hexadecimal conversion table

hex	0	1	2	3	4	5	6	7
8	−128	−127	−126	−125	−124	−123	−122	−121
9	−112	−111	−110	−109	−108	−107	−106	−105
A	− 96	− 95	− 94	− 93	− 92	− 91	− 90	− 89
B	− 80	− 79	− 78	− 77	− 76	− 75	− 74	− 73
C	− 64	− 63	− 62	− 61	− 60	− 59	− 58	− 57
D	− 48	− 47	− 46	− 45	− 44	− 43	− 42	− 41
E	− 32	− 31	− 30	− 29	− 28	− 27	− 26	− 25
F	− 16	− 15	− 14	− 13	− 12	− 11	− 10	− 9

hex	8	9	A	B	C	D	E	F
8	−120	−119	−118	−117	−116	−115	−114	−113
9	−104	−103	−102	−101	−100	− 99	− 98	− 97
A	− 88	− 87	− 86	− 85	− 84	− 83	− 82	− 81
B	− 72	− 71	− 70	− 69	− 68	− 67	− 66	− 65
C	− 56	− 55	− 54	− 53	− 52	− 51	− 50	− 49
D	− 40	− 39	− 38	− 37	− 36	− 35	− 34	− 33
E	− 24	− 23	− 22	− 21	− 20	− 19	− 18	− 17
F	− 8	− 7	− 6	− 5	− 4	− 3	− 2	− 1

See **addition**; **binary numbers**.

UDG   A system variable, address 23675. This 2-byte variable holds the address of the first byte of the data for the **user defined graphics**. At power-up a block of 168 bytes is reserved for UDG data – sufficient for all 21 graphics. If few graphics are needed, but the extra memory space would be useful, then move UDG. This can be done by changing the first byte – the second byte must always be 255. UDG can be moved up 8-bytes for every graphic that is not wanted. No matter how high you raise UDG, the first graphic will always be on 'A'.

ULA (Uncommitted Logic Array)   A special chip designed specifically for the Spectrum. It contains some of the video circuitry and input/

output devices.

update   Every filing and data-processing
program should have an update option, so that
data entered previously can be altered and
brought up to date. The updated version
should be saved separately and with a new
filename.

user defined graphics   A character
occupies an 8 by 8 grid of pixels on the screen,
and its definition is held in the memory as a
block of 8-bytes, each byte corresponding to
one line of the character.

To define your own characters, bytes must
be POKEd into the appropriate place in the
UDG area. The pattern can be given in binary
or in decimal, e.g.:

```
BIN 00001000 = 8
BIN 00001100 = 12
BIN 11111110 = 254
BIN 10000011 = 131
BIN 11111110 = 254
BIN 00001100 = 12
BIN 00001000 = 8
BIN 00000000 = 0
```

A simple FOR. . .NEXT loop will READ the design DATA into memory:

```
100  FOR r = 0 TO 7: REM 8 rows
110  READ pattern
120  POKE USR "A" + r,pattern
130  NEXT r
140  DATA 8,12,254,131,254,12,8,0
```

Graphics can be redefined at any point during a program, and if more than 21 are required at the same time, then the character set can be moved into RAM and redefined.

See **BIN**; **CHARS**; **memory saving**; **READ**.

user friendly A program or an operating system that is easy to understand and responds positively to errors.

USR A function (E Mode on **L**). 'USR address' refers to the **machine code** routine starting at that address. The routine can be called in three ways:

(1) PRINT USR address: this runs the routine, and prints the contents of the BC register on return to BASIC.

(2) LET variable = USR address: there the

code is called, but the BC contents are transferred to the variable, rather than being displayed.

(3) RANDOMIZE USR address: this simply runs the code, without passing any data back to BASIC.

When defining graphics, the variation 'USR "letter" ' gives the address at which the first byte of data for the graphic is to be stored. The letter must be in the range "A" to "U" – both capitals and lower case are accepted.

VAL A function (E Mode on ▉). 'VAL string' will give a numerical value for any number, or numerical expression in string form. VAL "2" = 2. VAL "3 * 4 + 5" = 17. If you wish to save memory, and do not mind the extra typing, it is possible to write all numbers in string form, and then evaluate them when needed.

```
LET a$ = "99": LET b$ = "33"
PRINT VAL a$ + VAL b$
```

**VAL$** A function (E Mode, SYMBOL SHIFT and ▉). This rather odd function strips the quotes off the outside of strings, but if it is to work, there must be a string left at the end. 'VAL$ "string" ' would return 'string', but would not work if the extra quotes were missing. 'VAL$ "a$" ', 'VAL$ " ""text"" "' would give valid results. 'VAL$ "word"' would not.

variable A named area of memory in which data can be stored, and from which it can be recalled using the variable name. The Spectrum uses several kinds of variables:

(1) Simple numeric: each will store a number in **floating point binary** form. The variable name must start with a letter, but can be of any length; e.g. a, age, z3.

(2) Simple string: each will store an unlimited number of characters in **ASCII code** form. The variable name must be a single letter followed by the dollar sign; e.g. a$, C$, z$.

(3) Number array: here a set of stores all have the same identification letter, but are referred to individually by subscripts; e.g. a(2,3), n(1,12). Each element of the array acts

as a simple numeric variable.

(4) String array: like number arrays, these have a single identification letter (+$) and use subscripts to refer to individual strings. Unlike simple strings, arrayed string variables have their length fixed when the array is dimensioned.

(5) Control: the variables in FOR-...NEXT loops are stored in a different way to other numbers, as the Spectrum needs to know not just the number, but also the start and end points of the range, and the increment value. Only single-letter names are permitted.

VERIFY A statement (E Mode, SYMBOL SHIFT and **R**). 'VERIFY' performed after 'SAVE' will check the quality of the recording. If the program or data is the same as the version held in the memory, then an 'O.K.' message will be displayed.

'VERIFY filename' checks a program. 'VERIFY filename CODE start, length' checks a block of code. 'Start' and 'length' can normally be omitted as the Spectrum will check against the original startpoint for the original length unless otherwise instructed. 'VERIFY filename DATA array()' checks an array.

SCREEN$ are difficult to verify, as the screen is normally overprinted with the SAVEing name during verification.

Most Spectrums will work reliably with most cassette recorders, so that verification is rarely necessary.

'VERIFY ✳"m";d;"filename"' verifies the basic program on microdrive 'd'. 'VERIFY ✳"n";x' verifies the BASIC program on the network station number 'x'.

X-axis The conventional term for the horizontal axis used in high-resolution graphics.

XOR A Z80 instruction mnemonic: 'XOR register' acts on the accumulator.

In an XOR operation the corresponding bits in two bytes are compared. If one bit is logic $\emptyset$ and the other logic 1 then the result is logic 1; otherwise the result is logic $\emptyset$. XORing a byte with 255 (11111111) has the effect of inverting (or flipping) its bits. Inverting a byte gives its complement, e.g.:

	DECIMAL	BINARY
	181	10110101
XOR	255	11111111
	74	01001010

See **truth tables**.

flag register

Mnemonic	Operand	Bytes	Clock cycle	S	Z		H		P/O	N	C
XOR	data	2	7	$	$		$		P	1	0
XOR	register	1	4	$	$		$		P	1	0
XOR	(HL)	1	7	$	$		$		P	1	0
XOR	(index registers +displacement)	3	19	$	$		$		P	1	0

Y-axis The vertical axis. *See* **X-axis**.

zero page addressing This addressing mode is specific to the instructions that exclusively operate in the first 256 bytes of memory, that is to say, **RST** instructions.

Z80A This version of the Z80 chip is the micro-processor at the heart of the Spectrum. It uses standard Z80 machine code, and differs from the Z80 only in that it is slightly quicker in performing some operations.

Z80 MNEMONICS In this list the following conventions are used:

    n   single-byte number as data or displacement

    nn   2-byte number or address

    (nn) byte in address given by number

    (RR) byte in address held in register pair specified

All instruction codes conform to certain patterns. Those using the single registers A,B,C,D,H,L and the bytes in HL, IX+n, IY+n are formed from a base number plus a reference number, e.g.:

ADC	BASE	A	B	C	D	E	H
	136	+7	+0	+1	+2	+3	+4
		143	136	137	138	139	140

ADC	BASE	L	(HL)	(IX+n)	(IY+n)
	136	+5	+6	221,+6,n	253,+6,n
		141	142	221,142,n	253,142,n

Where this pattern occurs it will be shown thus: CODE,pattern HEX+p DECIMAL+p.

MNEMONIC	HEX	DECIMAL
ADC A,pattern	88+p	136+p
ADC A,n	CE,n	206,n
ADC HL,BC	ED,4A	237,74
ADC HL,DE	ED,5A	237,90
ADC HL,HL	ED,6A	237,106
ADC HL,SP	ED,7A	237,122
ADD A,pattern	80+p	128+p
ADD A,n	C6,n	198,n
ADD HL,BC	09	9
ADD HL,DE	19	25
ADD HL,HL	29	41
ADD HL,SP	39	57
ADD IX,BC	DD,09	221,9
ADD IX,DE	DD,19	221,25
ADD IX,HL	DD,29	221,41
ADD IX,SP	DD,39	221,57
ADD IY,BC	FD,09	253,9
ADD IY,DE	FD,19	253,25
ADD IY,HL	FD,29	253,41
ADD IY,SP	FD,39	253,57
AND pattern	A0+p	160+p
AND n	E6,n	230,n
BIT – see below		
CALL nn	CD,nn	205,nn

MNEMONIC	HEX	DECIMAL
CALL C,nn	DC,nn	220,nn
CALL M,nn	FC,nn	252,nn
CALL NC,nn	D4,nn	212,nn
CALL P,nn	F4,nn	244,nn
CALL PE,nn	EC,nn	236,nn
CALL PO,nn	E4,nn	228,nn
CALL Z,nn	CC,nn	204,nn
CCF	3F	63
CP pattern	B8+p	184+p
CP n	FE,n	254,n
CPD	ED,A9	237,169
CPDR	ED,B9	237,185
CPI	ED,A1	237,161
CPIR	ED,B1	237,177
CPL	2F	47
DAA	27	39
DEC pattern	05+8∗p	5+8∗p
DEC BC	0B	11
DEC DE	1B	27
DEC HL	2B	43
DEC SP	3B	59
DEC IX	DD,2B	221,43
DEC IY	FD,2B	253,43
DI	F3	243

MNEMONIC	HEX	DECIMAL
DJNZ, d	10, n	16, n
EI	FB	251
EX AF, AF'	08	8
EX DE, HL	EB	235
EX (SP), HL	E3	227
EX (SP), IX	DD, E3	221, 227
EX (SP), IY	FD, E3	253, 227
EXX	D9	217
HALT	76	118
IM 0	ED, 46	237, 70
IM 1	ED, 56	237, 86
IM 2	ED, 5E	237, 94
IN A, (C)	ED, 78	237, 120
IN A, port	DB, n	219, n
IN B, (C)	ED, 40	237, 64
IN C, (C)	ED, 48	237, 72
IN D, (C)	ED, 50	237, 80
IN E, (C)	ED, 58	237, 88
IN H, (C)	ED, 60	237, 96
IN L, (C)	ED, 68	237, 104
INC pattern	04+8*p	4+8*p
INC BC	03	3
INC DE	13	19
INC HL	23	35

MNEMONIC	HEX	DECIMAL
INC SP	33	51
INC IX	DD,23	221,35
INC IY	FD,23	253,35
IND	ED,AA	237,170
INDR	ED,BA	237,186
INI	ED,A2	237,162
INIR	ED,B2	237,178
JP,(HL)	E9	233
JP,(IX)	DD,E9	221,233
JP,(IY)	FD,E9	253,233
JP,nn	C3,nn	195,nn
JP C,nn	DA,nn	218,nn
JP M,nn	FA,nn	250,nn
JP NC,nn	D2,nn	210,nn
JP NZ,nn	C2,nn	194,nn
JP P,nn	F2,nn	242,nn
JP PE,nn	EA,nn	234,nn
JP PO,nn	E2,nn	226,nn
JP Z,nn	CA,nn	202,nn
JR,n	18,n	24,n
JR C,n	38,n	56,n
JR NC,n	30,n	48,n
JR NZ,n	20,n	32,n
JR Z,n	28,n	40,n

MNEMONIC	HEX	DECIMAL
LD – see below		
NEG	ED,44	237,68
NOP	00	0
OR pattern	B0+p	176+p
OR n	F6,n	246,n
OTDR	ED,BB	237,187
OTIR	ED,B3	237,179
OUT – as IN codes +1, except . . .		
OUT (port),A	D3,n	211,n
OUTD	ED,AB	237,171
OUTI	ED,A3	237,163
POP AF	F1	241
POP BC	C1	193
POP DE	D1	209
POP HL	E1	225
POP IX	DD,E1	221,225
POP IY	FD,E1	253,225
PUSH AF	F5	245
PUSH BC	C5	197
PUSH DE	D5	213
PUSH HL	E5	229
PUSH IX	DD,E5	221,229
PUSH IY	FD,E5	253,229
RES – see overleaf		

MNEMONIC	HEX	DECIMAL
RET	C9	201
RET C	D8	216
RET M	F8	248
RET NC	D0	208
RET NZ	C0	192
RET P	F0	240
RET PE	E8	232
RET PO	E0	224
RET Z	C8	200
RETI	ED,4D	237,77
RETN	ED,45	237,69
RL pattern	CB,10+p	203,16+p
RLA	17	23
RLC pattern	CB,0+p	203,0+p
RLCA	07	7
RLD	ED,6F	237,111
RR pattern	CB,18+p	237,24+p
RRA	1F	31
RRC pattern	CB,08+p	237,8+p
RRCA	0F	15
RRD	ED,67	237,103
RST 00H	C7	199
RST 08H	CF	207
RST 10H	D7	215

MNEMONIC	HEX	DECIMAL
RST 18H	DF	223
RST 20H	E7	231
RST 28H	EF	239
RST 30H	F7	247
RST 38H	FF	255
SBC A,pattern	98+p	152+p
SBC A,n	DE,n	222,n
SBC HL,BC	ED,42	237,66
SBC HL,DE	ED,52	237,82
SBC HL,HL	ED,62	237,98
SBC HL,SP	ED,72	237,114
SCF	37	55
SET – see below		
SLA pattern	CB,20+p	203,32+p
SRA pattern	CB,28+p	203,40+p
SRL pattern	CB,38+p	203,56+p
SUB pattern	90+p	144+p
SUB n	D6,n	214,n
XOR pattern	A8+p	168+p
XOR n	EE,n	238,n

BIT, RES and SET mnemonics have the same structure: 'INSTRUCTION bit number, register, e.g.:

RES 6,(HL)
BIT Ø,A
SET 4,(IX+n)

The codes for the registers are the same as with the simple patterns.

A	B	C	D	E	H
+7	+0	+1	+2	+3	+4

L	(HL)	(IX+n)	(IY+n)
+5	+6	221,+6,n	253,+6,n

OP CODE = 203, Base + 8 $*$ bit number + p
Bases: BIT − 64; RES − 128; SET − 192.
e.g. BIT 3,A = 203,64 + 8 $*$ 3 + 7 = 203,95
        RES 5,(IX+n) = 221,203,n,128 + 8 $*$ 5
        + 6 = 221, 203,n,174

All BIT, RES and SET instructions are preceded by CB (203), except for those using the IX or IY registers, which begin with 221,203,n. . . or 253,203,n. . .

Load instruction codes follow certain rules. Here, as elsewhere, instructions using '(IX+n)' or '(IY+n)' are the same as those using '(HL)', except that they are preceded by '221' (for IX)

or '253' (for IY), and end with the number,
e.g.:

    LD A,(HL) = 126
    LD A,(IX+n) = 221,126,n
    LD A,(IY+n) = 253,126,n

Where the LD instruction is from one register to another, the code is formed using the standard pattern numbers with a base of 64:

    64 + 8 * p (destination) + p (source)
    LD D,H = 64 + 8 * 2 + 4 = 84 (54H)

Some instructions follow less obvious patterns:

LD (nn),A	32,nn	50,nn
LD (nn),BC	ED,43,nn	237,67,nn
LD (nn),DE	ED,53,nn	237,83,nn
LD (nn),HL	22,nn	34,nn
LD (nn),SP	ED,73,nn	237,115,nn
LD (BC),A	02	2
LD (DE),A	12	18
LD (HL),n	36,n	54,n
LD A,(nn)	3A,nn	58,nn
LD A,(BC)	0A	10
LD A,(DE)	1A	26

LD A,(HL)	7E	126
LD A,I	ED,57	237,87
		(I = index register)
LD A,R	ED 5F	237,95
		(R = refresh register)
LD A,n	3E,n	62,n
LD B,n	Ø6,n	6,n
LD BC,(nn)	ED,4B,nn	237,75,nn
LD BC,nn	Ø1,nn	1,nn
LD C,n	ØE,n	14,n
LD D,n	16,n	22,n
LD DE,(nn)	ED,5B,nn	237,91,nn
LD DE,nn	11,nn	17,nn
LD E,n	1E,n	3Ø,n
LD H,n	26,n	38,n
LD HL,(nn)	2A,nn	42,nn
LD HL,nn	21,nn	33,nn
LD I,A	ED,47	237,71
LD L,n	2E,n	46,n
LD L,I	6D	1Ø9
LD R,A	ED,4F	237,79
LD SP,(nn)	ED,7B,nn	237,123,nn
LD SP,nn	31,nn	49,nn
LD SP,HL	F9	249
LDD	ED,A8	237,168

LDDR	ED,B8	237,184
LDI	ED,AØ	237,16Ø
LDIR	ED,BØ	237,176